PENGUIN BOOKS — GREAT IDEAS

God is Dead. God Remains Dead.
And We Have Killed Him.

Friedrich Nietzsche

1844–1900

Friedrich Nietzsche

God is Dead.
God Remains Dead.
And We Have Killed Him.

Translated by R. Kevin Hill and Michael A. Scarpitti

PENGUIN BOOKS — GREAT IDEAS

PENGUIN BOOKS

UK | USA | Canada | Ireland | Australia
India | New Zealand | South Africa

Penguin Books is part of the Penguin Random House group
of companies whose addresses can be found at
global.penguinrandomhouse.com.

Part I is taken from *The Will to Power*, which was based on Nietzsche's
notebooks and published posthumously in 1901. Part II is taken
from *The Joyous Science*, first published in 1882.
This selection published in Penguin Books 2020

007

Translation of Part I copyright © R. Kevin Hill
and Michael A. Scarpitti, 2017
Translation of Part II copyright © R. Kevin Hill, 2018

Set in 12/15 pt Dante MT Std
Typeset by Jouve (UK), Milton Keynes
Printed and bound in Great Britain by Clays Ltd, Elcograf S.p.A.

A CIP catalogue record for this book
is available from the British Library

ISBN: 978–0–241–47284–2

Contents

Part I. Critique of Religion

All the beauty and sublimity which we have ascribed to real and imagined things, I will reclaim as the property and product of man: as his most eloquent apology. Man as poet, as thinker, as god, as love, as power – oh, the royal liberality with which he has lavished gifts upon things in order to *impoverish* himself and make *himself* feel wretched! His greatest feat of selflessness has been that he admired and worshipped, and knew how to conceal from himself that it was *he* who had created what he admired.

*

Contrary movement; the origin of religion. Just as the uneducated man of today believes that when he is angry, his anger is the cause, that when he thinks, his mind is the cause, that when he feels, his soul is the cause – in short, just as a number of psychological entities are still unhesitatingly recognized as causes, in a still naïve age the same phenomena were explained with the help of person-like entities. Man attributed the conditions which struck him as strange, captivating or overwhelming to being under the influence of a demon or witch, i.e. a person. Thus the Christian, the most naïve and backward man of today, ascribes hope, serenity and a sense of 'deliverance' to a psychological inspiration from God; as one accustomed to suffering and distress, the Christian would rightly regard feelings of happiness, exaltation and serenity as strange, and in need of some explanation. Among intelligent, strong and vigorous races it was primarily the epileptic who inspired the belief that a strange power was at work here; but also any similarly involuntary condition, like that of the zealot, of the poet, of the great criminal, or passions like love or revenge, are conducive to the invention of superhuman powers. An abstract condition is made concrete by being identified with a person, and when the condition occurs, it is claimed to be the effect of that person. In other words, in the psychological genesis of God, an internal condition is personified as its own external cause, in order for the condition to be the effect of something other than itself.

The psychological reasoning is as follows: when a man is suddenly and overwhelmingly affected with a *sense of power* (as is the case with all great passions) it excites a doubt in his mind as to whether his own person could possibly be the cause of such an astonishing sensation; he dares not think so, and thus he posits a *stronger* person, in this case a deity.

In summa, the origin of religion lies in an exaggerated sense of power, which strikes people as *strange*; and just like the sick man who, finding that one of his limbs feels heavy and peculiar, comes to the conclusion that another man must be sitting on it, the naïve *homo religiosus* divides himself up into *several people*. Religion is an example of the '*altération de la personnalité*'. He experiences something like a sense of awe and dread before himself . . . But likewise a sense of *extraordinary happiness* and *elevation* . . . Among the sick, a sense of health suffices to make one believe that God exists, that God is near.

*

The primitive psychology of the religious man. Man reasons that all changes are effects, and all effects are the effect of volition (any conception of 'nature' or of 'natural law' being entirely absent here) – that every effect has its agent. His primitive psychology consists in thinking that he himself is a cause only when he is aware of having willed something. As a result, powerful states convey to man the impression that he is *not* their cause, that he is *not responsible* for them. Such states arise involuntarily; consequently he cannot be their author. The unfree will (i.e. the consciousness of an involuntary change in our internal condition) requires the existence of an *alien* will.

In consequence, man has never dared to attribute all of his strong and startling moments to himself; he has always thought of them as 'passive', as 'suffered', as overwhelming. Religion is the outgrowth of a *doubt* as to the unity of the person; it is an *altération* of the personality. In so far as everything great and strong in man was thought of as *superhuman* and *alien*, man diminished himself; he divided himself into two parts, one very wretched and weak, the other very strong and startling, and set them in their separate spheres, calling the one 'Man' and the other 'God'.

And he has persisted in doing so: during the period of *preoccupation with morality* he did not interpret his lofty and sublime moral states as 'voluntary' or as the 'work' of the person. Even the Christian divides his personality into a weak and *mesquine* fiction which he calls Man and another fiction which he calls God (redeemer, saviour).

Religion has degraded the very idea of 'man'; its ultimate consequence is that all goodness, greatness and truth are superhuman, and are bestowed by grace alone.

*

A form of religion to create national pride. The theory of affinity was another way of lifting man out of the degradation brought about by the rejection of his own lofty and strong states as something alien to him. These lofty and strong states could at least be interpreted as the influence of our ancestors, with whom we are related and stand in solidarity; we grow in our own estimation by acting in accordance with the familiar standard they represent. This is an attempt on the part of noble families to reconcile their religion with their own sense of self-respect.

Transfiguration, temporary metamorphosis. Poets and seers do the same thing; they feel proud to have been *singled out* for the honour of such dealings, and place great value on not being regarded as individuals, but as mere mouthpieces (Homer). Yet another form of religion: God chooses, God becomes man, God dwells among men, bestowing great blessings; a local legend is presented as an immortal 'drama'. Man gradually takes possession of the loftiest and proudest states, of his works and deeds. Formerly, people believed that they honoured themselves by assigning responsibility for their loftiest deeds, not to themselves, but to God. The *involuntariness* of a deed was thought to give it greater value; at that time a god was taken to be its author . . .

*

Priests are actors who play the role of something superhuman which must be made manifest, be it ideals, or gods and saviours; they have an instinct for this sort of thing and have made it their vocation; in order to make all this as credible as possible, they must go as far as possible in assimilating themselves to their role; above all, their actor's cunning must obtain for themselves a *good conscience*, by the aid of which alone can they be truly convincing.

*

Origin of morality. The priest wants to establish that he is to be regarded as the highest type of man, that he reigns, even over those who possess worldly power, that he is invulnerable, unassailable . . . that he is the strongest power in the community, absolutely not to be superseded or underestimated.

The *means* he employs are as follows: he alone is all-knowing; he alone is virtuous; he alone has an indomitable will; he alone is, in a certain sense, God, and has his origin in the Godhead; he alone is the intermediary between God and others; the Godhead punishes every passing thought in opposition to the priest, and every disadvantage imposed on him.

Further means he employs include: the *truth* exists. There is only one way of obtaining it, and that is to become a priest. Everything which is good, in the social order, in nature or in tradition, can be traced back to the wisdom of the priests. The Holy Book is their work; the whole of *nature* is but an execution of its laws. No source of goodness exists apart from the priests. Every other kind of excellence, e.g. that of the *king*, is of an entirely different order from that of the priest.

In consequence, if the priest is to be the highest type of man, then the hierarchy of his virtues must constitute the hierarchy of value among men. *Study, detachment, inactivity, impassibility, imperturbability, solemnity*; the *opposite* of all this is found in the *lowest* breed of men . . . The inculcation of fear, the gestures, the hieratic manners, the excessive *contempt* for the body and the senses – the *unnatural* as a sign of the *supernatural*.

The priest has taught one kind of morality in order to be considered the *highest type* of man. He then conceives of the *opposite* type of man, the chandala, the outcaste, whom the priest now denigrates by every available means, so that the outcaste might serve as a *foil* to the order of castes. Similarly, his extreme fear in the face of *sensuality* is also due to the *realization* that sensuality is the most serious threat to the *order of castes* (i.e. to *order* in general) . . . After all, every 'more liberal tendency' in *puncto puncti* throws the marriage laws *to the winds*.

*

7

The philosopher *as the further development of the* priestly *type*. The philosopher comes from a long line of priests, and that is what he is to the marrow of his bones; even as a rival he is obliged to use the same weapons as the priests of his day; and like them he aspires [to] *supreme authority*. What is it that confers *authority* upon men when they wield no earthly power (no army, no *weapons*) whatsoever? In particular, how do they gain authority *over* those who *do* possess earthly authority and might? How can they inspire more awe than princes, conquering heroes and wise statesmen?

Only by inspiring the belief that they wield an even higher and greater power: the power of *God*. And because there is nothing else so powerful, everyone must *depend upon* the mediation and the service of the priest. They present themselves as indispensable *intercessors*. For them it is vital: (1) that people believe in their God, in the absolute superiority of their God; and (2) that there is no other direct access to God. The *second* condition alone gives rise to the notion 'heterodoxy'; the *first* gives rise to the notion of an 'infidel' (i.e. he who believes in *another* god).

*

'*Betterment*'. *A critique of the holy lie*. It is a part of the theory of every priesthood that a lie is to be allowed for the furtherance of pious purposes; the subject of this investigation is to what extent it is also a part of their practice. But philosophers, who share the same ulterior motives as priests, have also never failed to arrogate to themselves the right to lie whenever they have intended to take the direction of mankind into their hands, Plato first and foremost. The most impressive of these is the double lie, developed by the typically Aryan philosophers of the Vedanta, in which there were two systems that contradicted each other in all their main points, but which for educational purposes are detached from one another, completing and complementing each other.

The lie of the one is supposed to create a condition in which the other truth becomes *discernible* at all . . . *To what lengths* have priests and philosophers gone with the pious lie? Here we must ask what they require with regard to education, and what dogmas they are compelled to *invent* in order to satisfy these requirements?

First, they must have power, authority and absolute credibility on their side.

Second, they must have the whole course of nature in their hands, so that everything affecting the individual seems to be conditioned by their law.

Third, their power must have an even wider scope than that; they must exercise a control over those they have subjugated which is well-nigh invisible, by punishment in the hereafter, in the 'afterlife' – and, of course, by knowing the way and means of beatitude.

They have to remove the notion of a natural course of events, but as they are wise and thoughtful people they are able to *promise* that, through prayers or the strict observance of their laws, a multitude of effects naturally ensue . . . They can, moreover, *prescribe* a multitude of things which are perfectly reasonable – provided that they do not attribute this wisdom to empirical knowledge and experience, but instead to revelation, and the fruits of the 'most severe self-mortification'. The *holy lie* therefore pertains principally to the *purpose* of an act (the natural purpose of the act, its real reason, is rendered invisible, and a moral purpose, compliance with some law, service to God, appears in its stead). The *holy lie* pertains to the *consequence* of an act as well (the natural consequence is interpreted as something supernatural, and in order to produce a certain effect, the prospect is held out of still more uncontrollable supernatural consequences).

In this way a conception of *good* and *evil* is created which appears to be entirely detached from the natural notions 'useful', 'harmful', 'life-promoting', 'life-diminishing'; indeed, in so far as *another* life is conceived, it may even be directly *antagonistic* to a naturalistic conception of good and evil. In this way, the famous notion 'conscience' is finally created: an inner voice which does *not* evaluate an act by its consequences, but by its intention and conformity of that intention to the 'law'.

As a result, the holy lie has invented: a God who *rewards* and *punishes*, who endorses none other but the code of the priests, who sends no one but them into the world as His mouthpieces and plenipotentiaries; an *afterlife* in which the great punitive machine is intended to operate from the outset, and to this end the '*immortality of the soul*'; the *conscience* in man, as consciousness that good and evil are immutable, that when the voice of conscience recommends conformity with priestly precepts it is the voice of God Himself who speaks; *morality* as the *denial* of any natural course of events, as the reduction of every event to an event conditioned by morality, to moralization (i.e. the notion of punishment and reward), as pervading the world, as the only power, as *creator* of all change; *truth* as given, revealed and in concurrence with the teaching of the priests, as the condition for all salvation and happiness in this life and the life to come. In short, what price is paid for moral *betterment*?

The suspension of *reason* and the reduction of all

motives to hope and fear (reward and punishment); *dependence* on the tutelage of the priesthood, and on exactitude in the observance of formalities claimed to express a divine will; the implantation of a 'conscience' that substitutes a *false knowledge* for trial and error, as if it had already been determined what should or should not be done – which amounts to a sort of castration of the enquiring and progressive mind; in short, the worst *mutilation* of man one [can] imagine, done ostensibly to make man 'good'.

In praxi, all reason, the entire inheritance of wisdom, subtlety and foresight which the priestly canon presupposes, is subsequently reduced in an arbitrary manner to a mere *mechanism*; conformity with the law becomes an end in itself, and the highest one too, for that matter. *All the problems of life are solved*.

The whole conception of the world is besmirched with the notion of *punishment* . . . Owing to the fact that the *priestly* life is upheld as the *non plus ultra* of perfection, life itself is reconceived in order to defame and defile it . . . The notion 'God' represents an aversion to, and a critique of, life; it represents a condemnation of life itself . . . Truth itself is recast as the *priestly* lie; the pursuit of truth as the *study of the Scriptures*, as the means of becoming a *theologian* . . .

★

Towards a critique of the laws of Manu. The whole book rests upon the holy lie. Was it the good of mankind that inspired this whole system? Was this kind of man, who believes that every action is guided by *self-interest*, interested or not in imposing this system? What inspires a man to form the intention of improving the human race? How does one arrive at the notion of betterment? Here we find a kind of man, the *priest*, who considers himself the standard, the pinnacle and the supreme expression of the human type. He comes to the conclusion that others stand in need of 'betterment' by comparing them to himself. He believes in his own inherent superiority, and *intends* to be superior to them in actual fact: the cause of the holy lie is the *will to power* . . .

In order to establish his own supremacy, he must establish the supremacy of ideas which place a *non plus ultra* of power with the priesthood. He seeks power by the holy lie in recognition of the fact that he does not already possess it in a physical, military sense . . . The holy lie augments his power – and furnishes him with a new notion: 'truth'.

It is a mistake to assume that this is some kind of *unconscious* and *naïve* development, some kind of self-deception. It is not fanatics who invent such carefully considered systems of oppression . . . Cold-blooded premeditation was at work here, the same sort of premeditation in which Plato engaged when crafting his *Republic*. The political insight, 'he who wills the end, wills the means', is one about which legislators have always been perfectly clear.

We possess the classical model in its specifically *Aryan* form; we can therefore hold the most gifted and most sober-minded of men responsible for the most fundamental lie that has ever been told . . . It has been imitated almost everywhere, and thus we can say that *Aryan influence* has corrupted the world . . .

*

Moralities and religions are the principal expedient by which men can be moulded into any desired form, provided one possesses an abundance of creative power and can enforce one's creative will over long periods of time, in the form of legislation, religions and customs.

*

Religion as such has nothing to do with morality; but both descendants of the Jewish religion are *essentially* moral religions which issue precepts as to how one *should* live, and which enforce their demands with rewards and punishments.

*

From the very beginning, the Christian priest was the mortal enemy of sensuality; it is difficult to imagine a greater contrast to this attitude than the feeling of innocent anticipation, the feeling of solemnity with which the presence of sexual symbols [was experienced], e.g. by women in the most venerable cults of Athens. In all non-ascetic religions the act of procreation was regarded as inherently mysterious: a sort of symbol of perfection, and of mysterious intent – a symbol of the future (rebirth, immortality).

*

To us, belief is the strongest fetter, the most painful scourge – and the *strongest wing*. Christianity should have elevated the innocence of man to an article of faith – then men would have become gods: in those days believing was still *possible*.

*

The great lies in history. As if it were the *corruption* of paganism that paved the way to Christianity! Rather, it was the enervation and *moralization* of the man of antiquity that did so! The reinterpretation of natural impulses into *vices* had already preceded its appearance!

*

Religion as *décadence*; *Buddha versus 'the Crucified'*. Within the larger nihilistic movement, it is necessary to make a sharp distinction between *Christianity* and *Buddhism*. Buddhism is the expression of a *fine evening*, of a perfect sweetness and gentleness, a sort of gratitude for everything left behind; it lacks bitterness, disappointment and rancour. Finally, it possesses a superior, intellectual love; the purification of a physiology at cross-purposes with itself is behind it now, and it is resting even from this, though it is precisely from this that it derives its intellectual glory and its blazing sunset (it has its origin in the higher castes).

Christianity is a movement bearing all the marks of degeneracy, consisting of all sorts of refuse and waste; it is *not* the expression of the downfall of a race, but from the very beginning an aggregate of morbid elements which huddle together, which seek each other out . . . It is therefore *neither* a national phenomenon, *nor* is it due to the influence of some particular *race*; rather, it appeals to the disinherited everywhere; at bottom, it is an expression of rancour against all that is well-constituted and dominant, of the need for a *symbol* to represent a curse on everything well-constituted and dominant. Moreover, it is contrary to all *intellectual* movements, to all philosophy; it takes the part of idiots, and utters a curse against the intellect. It is full of rancour against those who are gifted, learned, intellectually independent, for it suspects that they are *well-constituted* and *dominant*.

*

The only way to refute priests and religions is to show that their errors have ceased to be *beneficial* – that they do more harm than good; in short, that their own 'demonstration of power' no longer holds good . . .

*

Christianity should not be confounded with that one root from which it takes its name. The other roots from which it has sprung have been far more powerful, more important in forming its nucleus, than this one. It does an unparalleled injustice to his holy name to identify it with such horrible forms of deformity and decay as the 'Christian Church', 'Christian faith', 'Christian life'. What did Christ deny? Everything that now goes by the name of Christian.

*

All the doctrines that Christianity requires us to believe, all its 'truths', are mere lies and deception, and exactly the opposite of what the Christian movement had been at first . . .

That which is especially Christian in the *ecclesiastical* sense, is *anti-Christian* from the outset; conformity to things and people instead of to symbols; conformity to history instead of to eternal truths; conformity to formulas, rituals and dogmas instead of to a practice, a way of life . . . To be Christian is to be perfectly indifferent to dogmas, worship, priests, churches and theology . . .

The practice of Christianity is no fantasy any more than the practice of Buddhism is: it is a means to happiness . . .

*

Jesus goes straight to the point: the 'kingdom of heaven' is in the heart, and he does *not* find the means of attaining it in Jewish observances; even the reality of Judaism itself (its need to preserve itself) counts for nothing with him; he possesses *inward* purity. Nor does he care about all the crude formulas relating to our communion with God: he opposes the whole doctrine of repentance and atonement; he shows us how to live so as to feel 'deified', and how we do not come to feel that way by repentance and contrition for our sins. *'Sins are of no importance'* is his principal judgement. In order to become 'divine', the main thing is that we be sick of sin; in this respect, therefore, the sinner is in an even better position than the righteous . . . Sin, repentance, forgiveness – all of these have no place here . . . that is the admixture of Judaism, or else it is pagan.

*

The 'kingdom of heaven' is within the hearts of men (about children it is said, 'for theirs is the kingdom of heaven'): heaven has nothing to do with being 'above the earth'. The kingdom of God does not 'come', in a chronological or historical sense, by the calendar, something that would be here one day, and not the day before; it is a 'change of heart in individuals', and thus something about which, at any given moment, one could say that its time has come, and that its time has not yet come.

*

Christian misunderstandings. The thief on the cross: when the criminal himself, suffering a painful death, judges 'the way this Jesus suffers and dies, without rebellion, without enmity, graciously yielding, this alone is right', he affirms the gospel; and with that, *he is in paradise* . . .

*

Jesus distinguished between a real life, a life in truth, and ordinary life; nothing could have been further from his mind than the crude nonsense of a 'Peter made immortal', of the eternally continued existence of a person.

What he fought against was *self*-importance, the importance attached to the 'person'; how could he have wanted to immortalize *that*? He likewise fought against the hierarchy within the community; he never promises reward in proportion to desert; how could he have meant punishment and reward in the afterlife!

*

The humour of the thing, the tragic humour, is that Paul re-established on a grand scale precisely what Jesus had nullified by the example of his life. And when at last the Church was completed, even the *existence of the state* received its sanction . . . NB. Paul took the rudiments of a new *peace movement* not unlike Buddhism, a possible cure for *ressentiment* which had arisen in the very focus of the epidemic . . . and transformed it into its opposite, a pagan mystery religion, which eventually learns how to get along with the entire *organization of the state* . . . which eventually wages war, condemns, tortures, swears and hates.

Paul's point of departure is the great majority who are prone to religious excitement, and their need for mysteries. He is looking for a *sacrifice*, a bloody phantasmagoria which may rival the images of a secret cult: God on the cross, the drinking of the blood, the *unio mystica* with the 'sacrifice'.

He is trying to forge a link between *sacrifice* (after the model of Dionysus, Mithras, Osiris) and *resurrection* (understood as the *continued existence* of the individual soul, after it has been absolved and blessed).

He needs to bring the notions of *sin* and *guilt* into the foreground: *not* a new way of life (as Jesus himself demonstrated and taught), but a new cult, a new faith, a faith in a miraculous transformation ('salvation' through faith).

He understood that *the pagan world* had *great need* for such a thing; to that end, he arbitrarily selected and newly accentuated certain facts from Christ's life and death, giving them an emphasis that was generally misplaced . . . and thereby essentially *nullified* Christianity in its original form . . .

Thanks to Paul, the attempt to do away with *priests* and *theologians* led to a new priesthood and theology – a *ruling* class and a *church*.

The attempt to do away with *self*-importance, the importance attached to the 'person', led to belief in an eternally existing 'personal identity', to concern about 'eternal salvation' . . . and to the most paradoxical exaggeration of personal egoism.

One can see what came to an end with the death on the cross. *Paul* appears as the demonic bearer of bad tidings . . .

*

The Church is precisely that against which Jesus preached and against which he taught his disciples to fight.

*

There is no God who died for our sins, no salvation through faith and no resurrection after death: this is all false coin when compared with true Christianity, and for which that sinister, pig-headed fellow [Paul] must be held responsible.

The *exemplary life* is one of love and humility, a life whose large-heartedness does not exclude even the lowliest; a life which formally renounces entitlement, self-defence and victory (in the sense of personal triumph); a life which has faith in a beatitude here on earth, in spite of hardship, opposition and death; a life full of forgiveness and devoid of wrath or scorn; a life which seeks no reward and is bound to no one; a life of the most spiritual and intellectual emancipation; a life in which pride is subordinated to voluntary poverty and service.

Once the Church had taken away the *whole of Christian practice*, and had expressly sanctioned life in the state, the kind of life which Jesus had opposed and condemned, it had to find the *meaning* of Christianity elsewhere: in the *faith* in incredible things, in ceremonial prayer, worship, feasts, etc. The notions 'sin', 'forgiveness', 'punishment', 'reward', which are all quite insignificant for, and almost *precluded* by, early Christianity, now came to the fore.

A dreadful mishmash of Greek philosophy and Judaism; asceticism; perpetual judgements and condemnations; hierarchy . . .

*

From the very beginning, Christianity has done nothing but transform the symbolic into *crudities*:

(1) The opposition between 'true life' and 'false life' is misunderstood as an opposition between 'an immanent life' and 'a transcendent life'.

(2) The notion 'eternal life', in opposition to an ephemeral, personal life, is misunderstood as 'personal immortality'.

(3) The brotherhood formed by the common partaking of food and drink according to the

Hebrew-Arabic custom is misunderstood as the 'miracle of transubstantiation'.

(4) The 'resurrection' is misunderstood as the entrance to the 'true life' in the sense of a physical 'rebirth', and hence a historical contingency which occurs sometime after death.

(5) The teaching about man in general, of the vital relationship between man and God, is misunderstood as being about the 'son of God', and hence about the 'Second Person of the Trinity' – and it is just that which is *done away with*: the filial relationship of every man, even the least among us, to God.

(6) Salvation through faith, namely, that there is no other way to become sons of God save through the *way* of *life* taught by Christ, is turned into its opposite: salvation through believing that there is some miraculous *redemption* from *sin* which is not accomplished by man but by Christ's act. To that end, 'Christ on the cross' had to be reinterpreted.

In itself, this death was hardly the most important part of his work . . . it was only another indication of how to behave in the face of authority, in the face of the world's laws . . . not defending oneself . . . *Therein lay the example.*

*

Conviction: on the psychology of Paul. For *Paul*, the inescapable fact is the death of Jesus, a fact that is in crying need of an *interpretation* . . . That an interpretation might be true or false simply never occurs to such people; one day a sublime possibility crosses their minds, 'His death *might* mean such-and-such', and without hesitation they conclude that it *does* mean such-and-such! An hypothesis is proved by the sublime *enthusiasm* it inspires in its originator . . . This is an example of 'the demonstration of power'; i.e. a thought's truth is demonstrated by its *effects* ('by their fruits', as the Bible ingenuously says); that which a man finds delightful, that for which a man sheds his blood, must be *true*.

In such cases, generally speaking, the sudden sense of power which a thought arouses in its originator is attributed to the thought itself – the thought seems to be intrinsically *valuable* – and since he knows no other way of honouring it than by calling it *true*, that is the first predicate he applies to it . . . How else could it be so effective? He imagines that the thought comes to him from a higher power, and if the power were not real, it could not be effective at all . . . The thought is regarded as *inspired*; the influence it exerts has something of the authority of the supernatural about it. A thought which such a

25

décadent finds irresistible, and to which he becomes completely addicted, is therefore 'demonstrably' *true*. None of these holy epileptics and visionaries had a fraction of the integrity, of the capacity for self-critique, which a philologist today brings to the reading of a text, or to the testing of an account of some historical event for accuracy . . . compared to us, such people are moral cretins.

*

Christianity's indifference as to *whether a thing is true* provided it is *effective* betrays an *utter want of intellectual integrity*. Everything is acceptable, including lying, slander or the most shameless hypocrisy, provided it serves to raise the temperature – until people 'believe'.

Christianity is a formal school in the means of indoctrination, i.e. *seduction*, means which include: a fundamental contempt for those spheres from which opposition might be expected (for reason, for philosophy and wisdom, for careful and sceptical investigation); outrageous praise and glorification of the doctrine, with continual reference [to the fact] that it was God (and not the apostle) who gave it to us; that it is not open to question, but is to be accepted on faith; that it is the most extraordinary grace and favour to receive such a doctrine of salvation; that it is to be received with the deepest gratitude and humility . . .

Christianity is always betting on the *ressentiments* which people of low condition feel against everything held in high esteem; what seduces them into accepting this doctrine is the fact that it is presented to them as the counter-doctrine to the wisdom of this world, to the powers of this world. Outcasts and unfortunates of every kind find it convincing; it promises blessings, advantages and privileges to the most humble and unimpressive; it incites these poor little foolish heads to fanaticism, filling them with unreasonable presumption, as though they were the point of everything, the salt of the earth –

As I said, one cannot sufficiently despise all of this. We have been spared the necessity of *criticizing the doctrine itself*; it suffices to consider the means it employs to know what it is with which we are concerned. In the whole history of the intellect there has never been a more brazen, barefaced lie, a more carefully considered piece of unworthiness, than Christianity – and yet this doctrine aligned itself with *virtue*, shamelessly availing itself of the whole *fascinating power of virtue* . . . it aligned itself with the power of paradox, with ancient civilization's taste for pepper and appetite for absurdity; it excited amazement and indignation; it provoked persecution and ill-treatment.

It is exactly the same kind of *carefully considered piece of unworthiness* with which the Jewish priesthood established its power and created its church . . .

One must be able to distinguish between that warmth of the passion called 'love' (resting on a foundation of ardent sensuality) and the thoroughly *ignoble character* of Christianity, as manifested in:

— its constant exaggeration and garrulousness;
— its lack of dispassionate intellectuality and irony (there aren't any bad wits, let alone any good ones);
— its instinctively unmilitary character;
— its priestly prejudices against masculine pride, sensuality, the sciences and the arts.

★

The contrary movement of religion; morality as décadence; the reaction of little people. Love affords the greatest sense of power. The task is to understand to what extent it is not man in general, but rather a certain kind of man that is speaking here. This should be more closely scrutinized. 'By receiving divine love we become divine, we become "children of God"; God loves us and wants nothing from us, save love';

that is, no morality, obedience or action produces the same sense of power and freedom as love does; we do nothing bad out of love – we do much more good than we would have done out of mere obedience and virtue. Herein lies the happiness of the herd, the sense of community in things great and small, a lively sense of unity perceived as the *be-all and end-all of life's experiences*. Helping and caring for others, being of use to others, constantly excites a sense of power; evident success and an expression of pleasure in doing so only serve to emphasize the sense of power; nor is there any lack of pride felt as a community, as the dwelling place of God, as the 'chosen people'. In fact, man has once again undergone an *alteration of personality*: this time it is his feeling of love that he calls 'God'. One must try to imagine the awakening of such a feeling as a sort of rapture, a strange speech, a 'gospel'; it was this novel experience which prevented him from attributing this love to himself; he thought that God was walking before him and was alive within him. 'God has come to man', the 'neighbour' is transfigured into something divine (in as much as he evokes a feeling of love in him). *Jesus became the neighbour* as soon as he was reconceived as the Godhead, as the cause which *excites a sense of power.*

*

On the psychological problem of Christianity. The driving force is resentment, popular revolt, the revolt of the unfortunates. (Things are different in Buddhism: it is not *born* of a movement which is filled with *resentment*. Buddhism combats resentment because it leads to *action*.) This party of peace understands that it must *abstain from hostility in thought and deed* if it is to distinguish and preserve itself. Herein lies the psychological difficulty which has prevented Christianity from being properly understood: the impulse which *created* it leaves it no choice but to fight with itself, as a matter of principle. If this movement of revolt is to have any chance of success, it must be as a *party of peace and innocence*; it instinctively understands that it can only prevail by being extremely mild, sweet and meek. Its *trick* is to deny and condemn the impulse whose expression it is, and always to make a great show of the opposite impulse, in word and deed.

*

The pretence of youth. We deceive ourselves if we imagine that the early Christians were a naïve and youthful people, as contrasted with an old culture; it is a superstition to think that in the lowest strata of society, where Christianity grew and took root, deep springs of vitality were welling up afresh; we fail to understand the psychology of Christianity when we take it to be the expression of the newly emerging youthfulness of a people or the strengthening of a race. On the contrary, it is a typical form of *décadence*: the moral pampering and hysteria of an unhealthy, heterogeneous population that has become weary and aimless. The strange company which gathers around this master at the seduction of peoples, well, the whole lot of them actually, belong in a Russian novel; all nervous disorders meet in them . . . the absence of employment, the instinctive belief that everything is nearing its end, that things are no longer worthwhile, and that contentment lies in *dolce far niente*. The strength and assuredness of the Jewish instinct, the tremendous tenacity of its will to live, its will to power, lies in its ruling class; the strata which were elevated by primitive Christianity are distinguished by nothing except instinctual exhaustion. On the one hand, they are sick to death of the world around them; on the other hand, they are really quite pleased with *themselves*.

*

Like a nobility which, having sprung from a particular soil and race, finally emancipates itself from these conditions and *goes in search of* kindred elements, Christianity may be regarded as a form of *emancipated Judaism*, in so far as it is:

(1) A church (i.e. a community) covering the same territory as the state, but as an unpolitical formation;

(2) A life, a discipline, a practice, an art of living;

(3) A religion in which an offence *against God* is the *sole* kind of transgression and the sole cause of any suffering at all, that is, a *religion of sin*, with a universal remedy for it. We can only sin against God; whatever wrongs are done to man should neither be judged nor called to account, unless it be in God's name. Similarly, every commandment (e.g. the commandment to love one another) is referred to God, and obeyed by men for God's sake alone. Herein lies great wisdom – the only way a greatly circumscribed life (such as that of the Eskimo) can be borne is with a peaceable and lenient disposition, which is why Judeo-Christian dogma turned against sin for the good of the 'sinner' . . .

*

The *moral* of the story is that the founder of Christianity had to pay dearly for having appealed to the lowest stratum of Jewish society and intelligence. The spirit in which such people formed their conception of him was determined by what they themselves understood . . . It was a real disgrace to have fabricated events of salvation, a personal god, a personal saviour, a personal immortality, and to have retained all the trifling 'personal' and 'historical' incidents of someone's life in a doctrine which denies the reality of everything personal and historical. The tale of salvation has taken the place of the symbolic 'now' and 'always', 'here' and 'everywhere', just as the miracle has taken the place of the psychological symbol.

*

I consider Christianity the most fateful and seductive lie that ever existed, as the great *impious lie*: I prune off every shoot and sprout from the stump of its ideal, no matter how well disguised they are; I take exception to any half or three-quarter measures with regard to it – there is no alternative here but war.

The *morality of little people* has been made the measure of all things: this is the most horrible kind of degeneration that our culture has hitherto exhibited. And this *kind of ideal* is still hanging over our heads . . . in the form of 'God'!!

*

However modest may be one's claim to intellectual integrity, when one comes into contact with the New Testament one cannot help experiencing an inexpressible revulsion. The sordid and unbridled insolence with which rank amateurs express the desire to participate in a discussion of the great problems, and what is more, claim the right to sit in judgement on such matters, knows no bounds. The sheer casualness with which the most intractable problems are spoken of there, as if they were not problems at all (e.g. life, the world, God, the purpose of life) but rather simple things which these little hypocrites fully understood, is nothing less than outrageous.

*

On the *denaturalizing of morality*. The petty little virtues of these gregarious animals by no means lead to 'eternal life'; and while it may be very shrewd to make a show of them – and themselves with them – for those who have eyes to see it nevertheless remains the most ridiculous of spectacles. A man does not in the least deserve special treatment, on earth or in heaven, just because he perfectly embodies the virtue of moderation . . . like some dear little lamb; even in the best cases, he remains only a dear, silly little ram with horns – provided he is not bursting with vanity like some kind of court chaplain and making a scandal of everything with his magisterial posturing.

Just look at the immense range of colours with which these petty little virtues are illuminated and transfigured here – as though they were the reflection of divine qualities.

The *natural* purpose and utility of every virtue is invariably concealed; a virtue is only valuable with regard to a *divine* command or model, or with regard to otherworldly and spiritual goods. (How marvellous! As if virtue were a question of '*the salvation of the soul*' rather than a way of using fine sentiments to make things here as 'bearable' as possible.)

*

Christianity in its original form would be tantamount to the *abolition of the state*: it prohibits oaths, military service, courts of justice, self-defence or the defence of a community, and distinctions between fellow countrymen and strangers; likewise it prohibits *social hierarchy*.

Christ's example: he does not resist those who do him evil (he prohibits defence); he does not defend himself; what is more, he 'turns the other cheek'. (To the question: tell us if you are the Messiah, he replies: 'From now on you will see', etc.) He forbids his disciples to defend him; he makes it clear that he could get help if he wanted to, but that he does not *want* to. Christianity would also be tantamount to the abolition of *society*: it favours all that society disregards, it grows out of that which is disreputable and condemned, out of leprosy in every sense; it thrives on 'sinners', 'publicans' and prostitutes; it is led by the most foolish of men (the 'fishermen'); it disdains the rich, the learned, the noble, the virtuous and the 'proper' . . .

*

New Testament. The war in the New Testament against the noble and the powerful, the manner in which it is prosecuted, reminds one of nothing so much as of *Reynard the Fox* and his methods; but anointed with priestliness and a resolute refusal to admit to itself how shrewd it is.

*

For once, read the New Testament as a *book of seduction*:

It commandeers *virtue*, instinctively aware that this is the way to have public opinion on one's side, admittedly an altogether modest *virtue*, which acknowledges the value of perfectly gregarious sheep (along with their shepherds) and nothing more; a little, affectionate, benevolent, helpful and enthusiastically pleased kind of virtue which to all appearances is perfectly unassuming – which sets itself apart from the 'world'.

The *absurd conceit* of the thing – as if the fate of

mankind revolved around them to such an extent that the congregation on the one hand is always to be regarded as right, and the world on the other is always to be regarded as wrong and reprehensible, and consequently to be rejected.

The *senseless* hatred it bears towards everyone in power, but which never goes so far as to disturb them! It shows a kind of *inward detachment* which outwardly leaves everything as it was (servitude and slavery); it knows how to make *everything* into an instrument in the service of God and virtue.

*

On the history of Christianity. The continual change of *milieu* means that Christian doctrine continually changes its *emphasis*. The favouring of *lowly* and *little* people . . . The development of *caritas* . . . The typical 'Christian' gradually comes to embrace all the things that he originally rejected (*the very rejection of which defined him as a Christian*). The 'Christian' becomes a citizen, a soldier, a magistrate, a worker, a merchant, a scholar, a theologian, a priest, a philosopher, a farmer, an artist, a patriot, a politician, a 'prince'; he takes up the same *activities* which he had abjured (self-defence, litigation, punishment, the swearing of oaths, discrimination between one people and another, deprecation, rage). *Christ himself preached* that the kind of life Christians now lead is ultimately the very life from which we should strive to *disentangle* ourselves ... The *Church* is just as much a part of the *triumph* of what is anti-Christian, as the modern state and modern nationalism ... The Church is the barbarization of Christianity.

*

How even 'the masters' could become Christians. A community (tribe, lineage, herd, congregation) instinctively regards all those conditions and desires to which it owes its preservation as intrinsically valuable, e.g. obedience, mutual aid, respect, moderation, compassion – and therefore suppresses everything that opposes or obstructs them.

Likewise, *rulers* (whether they are individuals or classes) instinctively patronize and distinguish those virtues which make the people whom they have subjugated *industrious* and *submissive* (conditions and passions which may be utterly different from their own).

The *gregarious instinct* and the *instinct of the rulers* concur in finding a certain number of conditions and qualities praiseworthy, but not for the same reason; the former do so out of direct egoism, the latter out of indirect egoism.

The *submission of master races* to Christianity is

essentially due to their recognition that Christianity is a *gregarious religion*, that it teaches *obedience*: in short, that Christians are more easily ruled than non-Christians. Even in this day and age the Pope, having some inkling of this, recommends Christian propaganda to the emperor of China.

It should also be added that perhaps no one is more strongly affected by the seductive power of the Christian ideal than those whose nature is to love danger, adventure and conflict; those who love anything *which involves putting themselves in peril*, which involves the possibility of attaining a *non plus ultra* of the sense of *power*. Think of Saint Theresa, surrounded by the instinctive heroism of her brothers; Christianity appears here as a form of dissipation of the will and of will-power, as a quixotic type of heroism . . .

*

War against the *Christian ideal*, against the doctrine of 'beatitude' and salvation as the aim of life, against the supremacy of the simple-minded, the pure in heart, the sufferers, the unfortunate, etc. (And anyway, what is God or faith in God to us now! 'God' today is merely a faded word, we no longer have the slightest notion what it means!) But, as Voltaire said on his deathbed: 'Do not speak to me of that man here!'

When and where did any considerable man bear

the least *resemblance* to the Christian ideal? At least in the eyes of those who are psychologists and triers of reins! Skim the pages of a copy of Plutarch; all of his heroes fall short of it.

*

It is ironic that some people believe that modern natural science has *vanquished* Christianity. Christian value judgements have *by no means* been vanquished. 'Christ on the cross' is still the most sublime symbol – even now.

*

Poverty, humility and chastity. These three are dangerous and slanderous ideals, but like poisons that are useful remedies for certain diseases, as were used e.g. in the Roman Empire.

All ideals are dangerous, because they debase and stigmatize actuality; they are all poisonous, but as temporary remedies, indispensable.

*

God made man to be happy, idle, innocent and immortal; our actual life is an existence filled with falsehood, apostasy and sin, a penal existence . . . Suffering, struggle, work and death are deemed objections to life, question marks placed after life, something unnatural, something that is not supposed to last, for which one requires – and *has!* – a remedy.

From Adam down to the present day, mankind has found itself in an abnormal condition. God Himself sacrificed His son for Adam's sin, to put an end to this abnormal condition; the natural character of life is a *curse*; to those who believe in Him, Christ restores to them a normal condition; He makes them happy, idle and innocent. But the world has not become fertile without toil; women do not bear children without pain; sickness has not ceased; the most devout are no better off than the infidels in this respect. All that has happened is that man has been made free from *death* and *sin*, assertions which admit of no proof and which, therefore, the Church asserts all the more firmly. 'He is free from sin,' it says, not through his own actions, not through a rigorous struggle on his part; rather, he is *ransomed* through the *act* of *deliverance* – and thus made perfect, innocent and heavenly . . .

The *true* life is merely a belief (i.e. self-deception, madness). The whole of struggling, fighting, splendour-filled, darkness-filled, real existence is only a bad and false existence; the task is to be *delivered* from it.

*

NB. NB. 'Man, innocent, idle, immortal and happy' – this notion, 'highest aspiration', must be criticized first and foremost.

Why should guilt, work, death and suffering (*and*, Christianly speaking, *knowledge* . . .) be *contrary* to the highest aspiration?

The lazy Christian notions 'beatitude', 'innocence', 'immortality' . . .

*

Ignorance in physiologicis. Apparently, the Christian has no nervous system – that might explain: his contempt and deliberate disregard for the demands of the body, and for any *discoveries* about the body; his assumption that this is in accordance with man's higher nature, and necessary *for the good of the soul*; his reduction of all general bodily sensations to moral values, as a matter of principle. The Christian thinks that illness itself is due to his moral status, whether as a punishment or as a test, or even as a state of salvation – a state in which man becomes more perfect than he could be in a state of health (Pascal's idea) – and under certain circumstances, voluntarily makes himself ill in order to attain it.

*

Of Christian practice. Down through the ages man did not know himself physiologically; even today he does not know himself. The knowledge that e.g. man has a nervous system (but no 'soul') is still the privilege of the best-informed. But man has not had the slightest suspicion that he did not know these things about himself. A man must be quite affable to be able to say: 'I do not know this', in order to be *content* with his own ignorance . . .

Suppose he is suffering or is in a good temper, he has no doubt that he could find the reason for his condition were he but to look for one . . . so he looks for it. In truth, he cannot find the reason, for he does not have even the slightest idea where to look . . . So what happens? . . . He mistakes the *consequence* of his condition, e.g. the success of a work undertaken in a good temper (and which was undertaken at bottom because his good temper had already given him the courage to do so), for its *cause*; *ecco*, the work must be the *reason* why he is in a good temper . . . As a matter of fact his success, in turn, had the same cause as his good temper: the happy coordination of physiological forces and systems.

He feels bad, and *consequently* is not finished with some worry, misgiving or self-examination . . . He really believes that his bad condition is the consequence of his misgivings, of his 'sins' or of his 'self-examination'.

But often, after profound exhaustion and prostration, he recovers. 'How is it possible that I feel such a sense of freedom and liberation?' 'It is a miracle which only God could have accomplished.' Conclusion: 'He has forgiven my sins' . . .

And that implies a practice: to encourage a sense of sin, in order to prepare the way for acts of contrition, it is necessary to reduce the body to a morbidly nervous condition. The method of doing this is well known. As one might imagine, no one suspects the necessary connection between these facts; since the mortification of the flesh is given a religious interpretation, it seems like an end in itself, whereas it is only a *means* of bringing about remorse, that morbid indigestion of the soul (with the aid of the '*idée fixe*' of 'sin', that chalk-line for hypnotizing hens).

The maltreatment of the body lays the groundwork for a series of 'guilty feelings', that is, for a general distress which *is ready to be furnished with an explanation* . . .

On the other hand, the method of 'salvation' emerges in a similar way: every kind of excess of feeling is provoked through prayer, bodily movements, gestures and oaths, and exhaustion ensues, often quite abruptly and often accompanied by forms of epilepsy. And after this condition of profound torpor comes the apparent recovery or, in religious parlance, 'salvation'.

*

Even if a reply to objections raised against the tenets of Christianity could not be given, Pascal held that in view of the *terrible* possibility that they were nevertheless true, it was in the highest degree prudent to be a Christian. As a sign of how much Christianity has lost its formidableness, today there are those other attempts at justification, to wit, that even if Christianity were a mistake, we still enjoy great advantages and benefits in the course of our lives from making this mistake; it therefore seems that we should uphold this belief for its *tranquillizing* effect – thus not out of fear of an imminent possibility, but rather out of fear of a life that has lost its charm. This hedonistic turn, the demonstration from *pleasure*, is a symptom of decline; it replaces the demonstration from *power*, the demonstration from the one truly shocking thing in the idea of Christianity, the demonstration from *fear*. Actually, with this interpretation Christianity approaches exhaustion: people are satisfied with a *narcotic* form of Christianity because they have neither the strength to seek, to struggle, to dare, to be willing to stand alone, nor the strength to espouse Pascalism along with its deep, brooding self-contempt, its belief in human worthlessness and its anxiety about 'possible damnation'. But a Christianity which before all else is supposed to tranquillize diseased nerves *hardly requires* the terrible solution of a 'God on the cross', which is why Buddhism is quietly gaining ground all over Europe.

★

People have failed to devote sufficient attention to the barbarous notions according to which Europeans still live. Case in point: the fact that they have been able to believe that 'the salvation of the soul' depended on a book! . . . And I am given to understand that this is believed to this day. What use is all this scientific education, critique and hermeneutics if the absurd interpretation of the Bible upheld by the Church has not yet stained us for ever red with shame?

★

Something to consider. The fatal belief in *divine providence* is easily the most *debilitating* belief there ever was, both practically and intellectually. But to what extent does it still persist under other guises? To what extent does Christianity as a tacit assumption and interpretation live on under the guise of such formulas as 'nature', 'progress', 'perfectibility' and

'Darwinism', or the superstition that there is a certain relationship between happiness and virtue, between unhappiness and guilt? That absurd *confidence* in the course of things, in 'life' and in the 'instinct of life'; that petty-bourgeois *resignation* which believes that if everybody did his duty *all* would go well – this sort of thing only makes sense on the assumption that things are directed *sub specie boni*. Even *fatalism*, the current form taken by our philosophical sensibility, is the result, albeit an unconscious one, of an *enduring* belief in divine providence. To wit, we think that how everything goes has nothing to do with *us*, and so we might as well let things take their own course, the *individual* being only a *modus* of absolute reality . . .

★

Consider the *losses* suffered by all human institutions, if we fasten upon a divine and transcendent, *higher sphere* in order to give these institutions a prior *sanction*. Once we have become accustomed to seeing their value in terms of this sanction (e.g. as in marriage) their *natural value is neglected*, and under certain circumstances *denied* . . . Nature gives offence in proportion as anti-nature – God – is given honours. 'Nature' becomes equivalent to 'contemptible', 'bad' . . .

The disastrous nature of a belief in *God as the*

embodiment of the highest moral qualities: all genuine values were thereby denied and held to be *worthless* as a matter of principle. Thus, the *anti-natural* ascended the throne, and with inexorable logic we arrived at the absolute requirement: *the rejection of nature.*

*

When I gaze upon the spectacle of Christian moral quackery, my compassion and contempt follow each other in rapid succession; sometimes I am outraged by it, as by a despicable crime. Here, error is made obligatory – a 'virtue' even – one takes matters in hand by failing to grasp them; the destructive instinct is systematized as 'redemption'; here, to operate is to eviscerate, to remove the very organs without whose energy a return to health is impossible. And, in the best of cases, one array of symptoms is exchanged for another, while the underlying malady remains uncured . . . And this pernicious nonsense, this systematized castration and rape of life, is considered sacred and inviolable; to live in its service, to be an instrument of this healing art, to be raised to the *priesthood*, makes one venerable, makes one sacred and inviolable oneself. The only possible author of such a supreme art of healing is the Godhead itself; the only way to understand salvation is as a revelation, as an act of grace, as an unmerited gift conferred upon the creature.

First proposition: psychological health is regarded as pathological, suspicious . . .

Second proposition: the prerequisite for a strong and prosperous life, strong desires and passions, is considered an objection to a strong and prosperous life.

Third proposition: everything which poses a threat to man, everything which might overmaster him and ruin [him], is evil and reprehensible and should be eradicated from his psyche.

Fourth proposition: man rendered harmless to himself and others, weak, prostrate in humility and self-effacement, aware of his weakness, in other words, man the 'sinner' – this is the most desirable type, and one which can even be *produced* by means of a little psychological surgery . . .

*

Let us see what 'the first Christian' proceeds to do with everything that he instinctively avoids: he *besmirches* and accuses the beautiful, the brilliant, the rich, the proud, the self-assured, the knowledgeable and the powerful – in sum, *all culture*; his intention is to deprive it of its *good conscience*. Sometime try reading Petronius immediately after reading the

New Testament: one can breathe freely again! One can blow away the damned air of hypocrisy!

*

Christianity. Previous attacks on Christianity have not been merely too cautious but altogether wrong-headed. As long as Christian morality was not felt to be a *capital crime against life*, its apologists had an easy time of it. The mere question of Christianity's 'truth', whether in regard to the existence of its God or the historical accuracy of the legend of its origin, not to mention its astronomy and natural science, is of secondary importance, as long as the question of the value of its morality is not touched upon. Is Christian morality *good for* anything, or is it a shame and a disgrace, despite all the holiness of its wiles? There are all kinds of ways of shielding Christianity from any attempt to determine its truth or falsity; and ultimately, the most credulous can always avail themselves of the logic of the incredulous, in order to give themselves the right to regard certain positions as irrefutable – that is, as *beyond* all possibility of refutation (the current expression for this clever dodge is 'Kantian critique').

Part II. God is Dead

NEW STRUGGLES

After the Buddha died, people showed his shadow for centuries afterwards in a cave – a monstrous and unearthly shadow. God is dead; but given the ways of men, perhaps for millennia to come there will be caves in which His shadow will be shown.

And we – we still have to subdue His shadow!

LET US BEWARE!

Let us beware of thinking that the world is a living being. To where would it spread? With what would it nourish itself? How could it grow and multiply? We have a pretty good idea what the organic is; and we are supposed to reinterpret something unspeakably derivative, late, rare and accidental, something we only perceive on the surface of the earth, into something essential, universal and eternal, as do those who call the universe an organism? That disgusts me. Let us beware of believing that the universe is a machine; it is certainly not constructed for any one purpose; we do it too much honour with the word 'machine'. Let us beware of presupposing that something as perfectly shaped as the cyclical movements of our solar system obtains at all times and places; indeed a glance at the Milky Way raises doubts as to whether there are not much rougher and more contradictory movements there, and even stars with eternally linear paths and the like. The astronomical order in which we live is an exception; this order, and the considerable time which it requires, has again made possible that exception of exceptions, the development of organic life. The overall character of the world, however, is from all eternity chaos; not in the sense of a lack of necessity, but rather in the sense of a lack of order, structure, form, beauty, wisdom and whatever else our aesthetically attractive human qualities are called. The failures are by far the most numerous, the exceptions are not the secret purpose; and the whole music box perpetually repeats what should never be called a melody – and finally the very expression 'failure' is already an anthropomorphism which implies censure. But how could we presume to blame or praise the universe! Let us beware of imputing to it heartlessness and irrationality, or their opposites; it is neither perfect, nor beautiful, nor noble, nor wishes to become any of these things; it by no means strives to emulate man! It is by no means subject to our aesthetic and moral judgements! It also has no instinct for self-preservation, indeed, no instincts whatsoever; it also knows no law. Let us beware of saying that there are laws in nature. There are only necessities: there is no one who commands, no one who obeys, and no one who transgresses. When you know that nothing is intentional, then you also know that nothing is accidental; for it is only where there is a world of intentions that the word 'accident' has any meaning. Let us beware of saying that death is the opposite of life. The living is only a species of the dead, and a very rare one at that.

Let us beware of thinking that the world perpetually creates what is new. There are no perpetually enduring substances; matter is as much an error as the god of the Eleatics. But when shall we have done with our caution and care? When will all these shadows of God no longer darken our understanding? When will we have completely demythologized nature? When may we begin to *naturalize* ourselves by means of the pure, newly discovered, newly redeemed nature?

MORAL SCEPTICISM IN CHRISTIANITY

Even Christianity has made a great contribution to enlightenment: it taught moral scepticism in a very forceful and effective manner, accusing and deprecating with untiring patience and subtlety; it annihilated every individual's belief in his own 'virtue'; it wiped off the face of the earth those celebrated prigs of whom there were so many in antiquity, men who, confident in their own perfection, strutted about with all the dignity of a matador. When we now read antiquity's books about morality, for example those of Seneca or Epictetus, after being trained in this Christian school of scepticism, we feel an amused sense of superiority, and are full of hidden insights and overviews; it seems to us as if a child were speaking to an old man, or a beautiful young enthusiast to La Rochefoucauld: we know better what virtue is! Eventually, however, we have also applied this very scepticism to all *religious* states and processes, such as sin, repentance, grace and holiness, and have allowed the worm to burrow so deeply that we now have the same sense of subtle superiority and insight while reading any Christian books: we also know better what the religious sentiments are! And the time has come to know them well, to describe them well, for the pious of the old faith are also dying out – let us save their likeness and type, if only for the sake of knowledge!

KNOWLEDGE MORE THAN A MEANS

Even *without* the passion for knowledge, science would still be promoted; science has hitherto grown and matured without it. The belief in science, the prejudice in its favour which now dominates every state in Europe (just as it had once dominated the Church), rests, in essence, on the fact that this unconditional inclination and impulse is so rarely present, and that science is *not* considered a passion, but a condition and an 'ethic'. Indeed, for some, curiosity, the *amour-plaisir* of knowledge, is enough; for others, *amour-vanité* and force of habit, along with the ulterior motive of honours and bread, are enough; for many, an abundance of leisure, with nothing better to do than to read, collect, organize, observe and recount, is enough – their 'scientific impulse' is *boredom*. Once, Pope Leo X (in his letter to Beroaldus) sang the praises of science: he described it as the most beautiful ornament and the greatest glory of human life, a noble occupation in prosperity or adversity. 'Without it,' he says finally, 'all human undertakings should be deprived of a firm footing – even with it they are changeable and uncertain enough!' But in the end this somewhat sceptical pope, like all other ecclesiastical apologists for science, keeps his counsel about it. While we may discern in his words a willingness to place science even above the arts, which is remarkable enough in so great a patron of them, ultimately it is only graciousness which prevents him from mentioning what he places high above even science: the 'revealed truth' and the 'eternal salvation of the soul' – and what are ornament, glory, preservation, or life's uncertainties to him, compared to that? 'Science is something secondary, nothing ultimate or unconditional; it is no object of passion' – this remained Leo's judgement: the actual Christian judgement about science! In antiquity, the appreciation of science and the sense of its dignity were diminished by the fact that, even among its most ardent disciples, the pursuit of *virtue* came first. People believed that they had given knowledge the highest praise when they celebrated it as the best means to virtue. It is something new in history that knowledge wants to be more than a means.

IN THE HORIZON OF THE INFINITE

We have left dry land and put out to sea! We have burned the bridge behind us – what is more, we have burned the land behind us! Well, little ship, look out! Beside you is the ocean. True, it does not always roar, and sometimes it is spread out like silk and gold and a gentle reverie, but there will be hours when you realize that it is infinite, and that there is nothing more terrible than infinity. Oh, poor bird that felt free, and now beats against the bars of this cage! Alas, if homesickness should befall you, as if there had been more *freedom* there – when there is no longer any 'land'!

THE MADMAN

Have you not heard of that madman who lit a lantern in the bright morning light, ran to the marketplace and shouted incessantly, 'I seek God! I seek God!'? As there were many people standing together who did not believe in God, he caused much amusement. 'Is He lost?' asked one. 'Did He wander off like a child?' asked another. 'Or is He hiding? Is He afraid of us?' 'Has He gone to sea? Has He emigrated?' And in this manner they shouted and laughed. Then the madman leaped into their midst, and looked at them with piercing eyes and cried, 'Where did God go? I will tell you! *We have killed Him* – you and I! We are all His murderers! But how did we do this? How were we able to drink up the sea? Who gave us the sponge to wipe away the whole horizon? What did we do when we unchained this earth from its sun? Where is it heading? Where are we heading? Away from all suns? Are we not constantly falling? Backwards, sidewards, forwards, in all directions? Is there still an above and below? Are we not straying as through an infinite nothingness? Do we not feel the breath of empty space? Has it not become colder? Is night not falling evermore? Mustn't lanterns be lit in the morning? Do we hear nothing yet of the noise of the gravediggers who are burying God? Do we smell nothing yet of the divine putrefaction? For even gods putrefy! God is dead! God remains dead! And we have killed Him! How shall we, the most murderous of all murderers, ever console ourselves? The holiest and mightiest thing that the world has ever known has bled to death under our knives – who will wash this blood clean from our hands? With what water might we be purified? What lustrations, what sacred games shall we have to invent? Is not the greatness of this deed too great for us? Must we not become gods ourselves, if only to appear worthy of it? There has never been a greater deed – and because of it, whoever is born after us belongs to a higher history than all history hitherto!'

Here the madman fell silent and looked again at his listeners; they too were silent and stared at him, baffled. At last he threw his lantern on the ground, so that it broke into pieces and went out. 'I have come too early,' he then said, 'this is not yet the right time. This tremendous event is still on its way and headed towards them – word of it has not yet reached men's ears. Even after they are over and done with, thunder and lightning take time, the light of the stars takes time, and deeds too take time, before they can be seen and heard. This deed is further away from them than the farthest star – *and yet they have done it themselves!*'

It is said that on that very day, the madman made his way into various churches, and there intoned his requiem *aeternam deo*. When led out and called to account, he always replied, 'What are these churches now, if not the tombs and sepulchres of God?'

MYSTICAL EXPLANATIONS

Mystical explanations are considered deep; the truth is that they are not even shallow.

AFTER-EFFECT OF THE MOST ANCIENT RELIGIOSITY

Each thoughtless person believes that the will is uniquely effective, that volition is something simple, absolutely given, underived and intrinsically intelligible. He is convinced that when he does anything, for example delivers a blow, it is he who strikes, and that he struck because he *intended* to strike. He does not notice a problem here; rather, the experience of *volition* is sufficient not only to persuade him that there is such a thing as cause and effect, but to instil in him the belief that he *understands* that relationship. Of the mechanism that lies behind the event, and the hundreds of complex and subtle activities which must transpire before the strike can take place, and likewise the inability of the will to achieve even the smallest portion of them by itself – of all this he knows nothing. To him, the will is a magically effective power: the belief in volition as the cause of effects is the belief in magically effective powers. Now originally, whenever man saw an event take place, he believed that a will was the cause, and that persons, volitional beings, were somewhere in the background, bringing it about – the very idea that a mechanism was involved was far from his mind. But because for immense periods of time man only believed in persons (and not in matter, forces, things and so on), the belief in cause and effect has become his fundamental belief which he applies to everything that happens – even now he still does so instinctively, acceding to an atavistic belief of the oldest pedigree. The propositions 'no effect without a cause' and 'every effect is also a cause' appear to be generalizations of much more circumscribed propositions, to wit, 'where there are effects, there are acts of volition', 'there can only be effects on volitional beings', 'where there are effects on volitional beings, these are never just purely and passively suffered with no further effects ensuing from them, but rather, every form of suffering at the same time stimulates the will (to activity, defence, revenge or retribution)'. In the early history of mankind, the more general and the more circumscribed propositions were *identical*, the former were not generalizations of the latter, but rather the latter were meant to *exemplify* the former.

Schopenhauer, with his assumption that being is will, has enthroned a primitive mythology; he seems never to have attempted an analysis of the will, because like everyone he *believed* in the simplicity and immediacy of all volition – while volition is such a well-coordinated mechanism that it frequently escapes all but the most penetrating of observers. Against him, I offer the following propositions. First, in order for the will to arise, an impression of pleasure and pain is necessary. Second, the fact that a vehement stimulus is perceived as pleasure or pain is a matter of the *interpreting* intellect, which for the most part operates unconsciously; one and the same stimulus may be interpreted as pleasure or pain. Third, it is only in intellectual beings that there is pleasure, pain and will; the vast majority of organisms have nothing of the kind.

THE VALUE OF PRAYER

Prayer was invented for those people who never have any thoughts of their own, and to whom spiritual exaltation is unknown, or at least passes unnoticed; what are these people to do in holy places and in those important situations in life where quiet and dignity of some kind are required? So that they at least do not *disturb* others, the wisdom of all founders of religions great and small has been to commend to them formulae of prayer which involve a protracted mechanical labour of the lips, associated with both an effort of the memory and a regular, fixed posture of hands, feet and eyes! They may then, like the Tibetans, ruminate on their '*Oṃ maṇi padme hūṃ*' over and over; or, as in Benares, count on their fingers the name of the god Ram Ram Ram (and so on, with or without grace); or honour Vishnu with the recitation of his thousand names, or Allah with his ninety-nine; or make use of prayer wheels and rosaries – the main thing is that they are in a fixed position for a time while performing this labour, and present a tolerable appearance; their manner of prayer was invented for the benefit of the pious who have thoughts and exaltations of their own. But even the latter have their weary hours when it does them good to have recourse to a series of venerable words and sounds and a mechanical piety to go with them. But supposing that these rare men – and in every religion, the religious man is an exception – know how to help themselves, the poor in spirit do not, and to forbid them their prayerful prattle would mean to take their religion away from them, a fact which Protestantism makes more and more obvious all the time. What religion wants from such people is that they should *keep still* with their eyes, hands, legs and every other part of their bodies; thus for a time they become beautiful to behold, and – more nearly human.

THE CONDITIONS FOR GOD

'God Himself cannot do without wise men,' said Luther, and not without reason; but 'Still less can God do without unwise men' – that is something the good Luther did *not* say!

A DANGEROUS DETERMINATION

The Christian determination to find the world ugly and bad has made the world ugly and bad.

CHRISTIANITY AND SUICIDE

From the very beginning, Christianity has taken advantage of the tremendous longing for suicide as an instrument of power; it permitted only two forms of suicide, invested them with the highest dignity and the highest hopes, and forbade all others in a dreadful manner. But martyrdom, and the gradual disembodiment of the ascetic, were allowed.

AGAINST CHRISTIANITY

It is no longer our reason which decides us against Christianity, but our taste.

PRINCIPLES

An unavoidable hypothesis of which mankind must avail itself again and again, is in the long run more powerful than the best-believed belief in something untrue (like Christian belief). In the long run: here, that means a hundred thousand years.

ORIGIN OF SIN

Sin, as it is now experienced wherever Christianity prevails or once prevailed, is a Jewish sentiment and a Jewish invention; and with respect to this background, which all Christian morality shares, Christianity was in fact bent on 'Judaizing' the whole world. To what an extent it succeeded at this in Europe is most keenly felt in the degree to which we find Greek antiquity – a world without the sense of sin – strange even now, despite our favourable attitude towards assimilating and incorporating it, something which whole generations and many distinguished individuals have not lacked. 'Only when you *repent* is God gracious to you' – a Greek would have found this laughable or offensive; he would say, 'slaves may harbour such sentiments'. We are to imagine here a mighty, indeed an almighty being, who is nevertheless prone to vengeance; his power is so great that no injury can be inflicted upon him except where a point of honour is involved. Every sin is an affront to his dignity, a *crimen laesae majestatis divinae* – and nothing more! Contrition, degradation, grovelling – this is the one and only condition with which his grace is associated; it leads to the restoration of his divine honour! Whether or not some other injury is done by the sin, whether or not the seeds of some profound and growing calamity are sown by it, which, like a disease, takes hold of one man after another and squeezes the life out of him, this vainglorious Oriental potentate in heaven is blithely indifferent; sin is an offence against him, not against mankind! And when God bestows His grace upon a man, He also bestows upon him this blithe indifference to the natural consequences of sin. God and mankind are regarded here as so separated, as so opposed, that in essence sin against the latter is entirely impossible – every deed should be considered *only with a view to its supernatural consequences*, not its natural ones: that is how Jewish sentiment would have it, for Jewish sentiment regards everything natural as inherently unworthy. The *Greeks*, on the other hand, seemed to think that sacrilege too could have dignity – even theft, as with Prometheus, even the slaughter of cattle as the expression of an insane jealousy, as with Ajax; in their need to impute some dignity to sacrilege, to make dignity at least some part of it, they invented *tragedy* – an art and a pleasure which, despite all their poetic gifts and their tendency towards the sublime, remained profoundly alien to the Jews.

SPOKEN IN PARABLE

A Jesus Christ was only possible in a Jewish landscape – I mean a landscape over which the gloomy and sublime thundercloud of Jehovah's wrath continually hung. Here alone would a sudden and unexpected ray of sunshine that penetrates the horribly constant and pervasive daylight darkness be regarded as a miracle of 'love', as the light of the most unmerited 'grace'. Here alone could Christ dream of his rainbow and his celestial ladder on which God descended to man; everywhere else the clear weather and sunshine were considered regular and everyday occurrences.

CHRIST'S ERROR

The founder of Christianity thought that people suffered from nothing so much as from their sins – that was his error, the error of someone who felt himself to be without sin, and who thus lacked experience in this respect! And so his soul was filled with that prodigious, fanciful pity for a particular kind of distress that was rare even among his own people, the very people who invented sin in the first place!

But Christians have always known how to provide their master with a justification after the fact; they hallowed his error by making it become the 'truth'.

COLOUR OF THE PASSIONS

For men like the Apostle Paul, it is a part of their nature to have an evil eye for the passions; they come to be acquainted with only the filthy, perverted and pathetic aspects of them – their ideal impulse, therefore, strives for the annihilation of the passions; they see the divine as completely dispassionate. The Greeks, in a manner quite different from Paul and the Jews, directed their ideal impulse precisely towards the passions, and loved, elevated, gilded and deified them; apparently, they not only felt happier when passionate, but more pure and more divine than ordinarily.

Well, what about the Christians? Were they not trying to become Jews? Is that not what they became?

TOO JEWISH

If God wanted to become the object of our love, then He ought to have forgone judging and justice first – for a judge, even a merciful one, is no object of love.

The founder of Christianity displayed an insufficiently refined sensibility in these matters – being a Jew.

TOO ORIENTAL

What? A God who loves men provided they believe in Him, and who casts terrible glances and hurls terrible threats at anyone who does not believe in this love? What? A qualified love as the feeling of an almighty God? A love which cannot even master a sense of honour and a petulant desire for revenge? How terribly Oriental it all is! 'If I love you, what concern is that of yours?' is already a sufficient criticism of the whole of Christianity.

INCENSE

Buddha says: 'Do not flatter your benefactor!' Repeat this saying in a Christian church – and it immediately cleanses the air of everything Christian.

THE GREATEST ADVANTAGE OF POLYTHEISM

For the individual to establish his *own* ideal and derive from it his own laws, his own pleasures and his own rights – in the past that was probably regarded as the most monstrous of all human aberrations, and as inherently idolatrous; in fact, the few who have dared to do so have always needed to apologize to themselves, usually in the following manner: 'Not I! Not I! But rather *a god* working through me!' It was in the wonderful art and ability to create gods – in polytheism – that this impulse could discharge itself, that it purified, perfected and ennobled itself; for originally this impulse was rather commonplace and unattractive, not unlike stubbornness, rebelliousness or envy. Formerly, hostility towards this desire for an ideal of one's own was the law of every morality. There was only one type and standard: 'man' – and every people believed itself to be this type, to be in *possession* of this standard. But in a distant heaven above and beyond oneself, one could discern a *multiplicity of standards*; to worship a particular god was not to deny or blaspheme against the other gods! It was here that individuals were first permitted, that the rights of individuals were first honoured. The invention of gods, heroes and superhuman beings of all kinds, as well as of quasi-human and subhuman beings – dwarfs, fairies, centaurs, satyrs, demons, devils – was an inestimable preliminary exercise in upholding the interests and prerogatives of the individual: the freedom one allowed a god with respect to other gods, one eventually gave to oneself with respect to laws, customs and neighbours. Monotheism, by contrast, is the inexorable consequence of the doctrine that there is only one type of man, and only one standard appropriate to him – and therefore the belief that there can be only one god for him, apart from whom there are only false gods. Such a conception was perhaps the greatest danger confronting mankind so far, because it threatened man with the same stagnation at which most other species of animals have already arrived, in that all of them believe in one type of animal and one ideal for their species, and have conclusively translated this morality of custom into flesh and blood. In polytheism, man's free-thinking and 'poly-thinking' is prefigured – to wit, his ability to create for himself new eyes, his own eyes, eyes which are ever newer, ever more his own. For this reason, man is the only animal for whom there are no eternal horizons or perspectives.

RELIGIOUS WARS

The thing in which the masses have displayed the greatest degree of progress hitherto is religious war; for it proves that the masses have begun to treat concepts with respect. Religious wars arise only when common reason has been refined by disputes between sects over the finer points of doctrine; so that even the rabble begins to quibble and regards trifles as important, even considering it possible that the 'eternal salvation of the soul' may hang on small differences between concepts.

GERMAN HOPES

Let us not forget that the names of peoples are usually epithets. The Tartars, for example, are called 'the dogs' – thus were they christened by the Chinese. 'Deutschen' (Germans) originally meant 'the heathen', which is what the Goths after their conversion called the great mass of their unbaptized kinsmen, as indicated by their translation of the Septuagint, in which the heathen are referred to with the word which in Greek means 'the nations': see Ulfilas.

It might still be possible for the Germans to make an honorific out of the old epithet, by becoming the first *non-Christian* nation of Europe; it does them honour that Schopenhauer thought this a task for which they were eminently suited. Were they to do so, then the work of *Luther* would be brought to completion, for he taught them to be un-Roman, and to say: 'Here *I* stand! *I* cannot do otherwise!'

WHERE REFORMATIONS ORIGINATE

At a time when the Church was highly corrupt, it was least corrupt in Germany, which is why the Reformation originated there, as an indication that even the beginnings of corruption were felt to be intolerable. Comparatively speaking, no people had ever been more Christian than the Germans of Luther's day; in Germany the bloom of Christian culture was ready to burst forth with hundredfold glory – only one more night was needed, but this one night brought the storm which put an end to everything.

THE FAILURE OF REFORMATIONS

It is a testimony to the superior culture of the Greeks that even in quite early times, several attempts to found new Greek religions failed; it suggests that from the very beginning, there must have been many different kinds of individuals in Greece, whose various kinds of distress could not be remedied by a single prescription of faith and hope. Pythagoras and Plato, perhaps even Empedocles, and, already much earlier, the Orphic rhapsodists, set out to found new religions; and the first two in particular had such natural gifts in this regard, not to mention the temperament and disposition for it, that their failure is nothing short of astonishing: all that they accomplished was to found sects. Every time that the reformation of an entire people fails and only sects rear their heads, we may infer that the people already contained various kinds of men, and had begun to break free from the coarser gregarious instincts and from the morality of custom – a condition fraught with significance, one in which everything remains in a state of suspense, a condition which we are accustomed to disparage as one of moral corruption and decline, but which in fact prefigures the ripening of the egg and the imminent breaking of the eggshell. The fact that Luther's Reformation succeeded in the North is a sign that Northern Europe had lagged behind the South, and as yet was only acquainted with needs of nearly the same kind and colour; and there would have been no conversion to Christianity in Europe at all if the culture of antiquity in the South had not been gradually barbarized by an excessive admixture of Germanic barbarian blood, and thereby forfeited its cultural superiority. The more general and absolute the influence of an individual, or the idea of an individual, the more similar and lowly must be the mass upon which it is exercised; while the opposing efforts betray opposing internal requirements, which also wish to prevail and gratify themselves. Conversely, one may always infer that a culture is actually superior when powerful and ambitious natures produce only a small and sectarian effect; this also applies to the individual arts and the fields of knowledge. Where there is ruling, there are masses, and where there are masses, there is a need for slavery. Where there is slavery, individuals are but few, and have the gregarious instincts and the conscience against them.

CRITICISM OF SAINTS

If we want to have a virtue, is it really necessary to have it in its most brutal form? This is how the Christian saints wanted and needed their virtues. The only thing which rendered their lives endurable was the thought that everyone would be overwhelmed with a sense of self-contempt at the sight of their virtue. A virtue with such an effect I call brutal.

OF THE ORIGIN OF RELIGION

Metaphysical need is not the origin of religions, as Schopenhauer would have it, but only a *later offshoot* of them. Under the influence of religious ideas we have become accustomed to the conception of 'another world' that lies behind, beneath or beyond our own, and feel an uncomfortable sense of emptiness and privation as a result of the destruction of our religious delusions – and 'another world' springs from this feeling once more, only now it is no longer a religious world, but a metaphysical one. However, that which led to the assumption of 'another world' in primitive times was *not* a drive or a need, but a kind of intellectual confusion, an *error* in the interpretation of certain natural processes.

THE GREATEST CHANGE

The light in which we view things, the colours which we lend to them have all changed. We no longer quite understand how men of old understood the most familiar and commonplace things – for example, daytime and wakefulness; because of their belief in dreams they viewed wakefulness in a different light. And likewise the whole of life, with its reflection of death and death's significance; our 'death' is an altogether different death. All experiences shone differently, because a god shone forth from them; all decisions and glimpses of the distant future as well, because they had oracles, and secret portents, and believed in prophecy. 'Truth' was perceived differently, because formerly a madman could be regarded as its mouthpiece – something which makes *us* shudder or laugh. Every injustice made a different impression, because one feared divine retribution, and not only a civil penalty or a bad reputation. What was joy in an age when one believed in the devil and tempter! What was passion when one saw demons lurking everywhere! What was philosophy itself when doubt was felt to be a transgression of the most dangerous kind, and indeed as a crime against eternal love, as distrust of everything good, lofty, pure and merciful!

We have lent new colours to things, we are constantly painting them anew – but what is our more youthful artistry when compared with the *glorious palette* of those Old Masters! I mean those men of old, ancient mankind.

HOMO POETA

'To the extent that it is finished, I have single-handedly made this tragedy of tragedies; I have entangled morality with existence so tightly that only a god could unravel them again – as Horace demands! Now in the fourth act I have killed all the gods – in the name of morality! What is to become of the fifth act? Where am I to find a tragic resolution? Should I begin to consider a comic resolution?'

THE MOST INFLUENTIAL

When a man resists the whole spirit of his age, stops it at the gate and calls it to account, that *must* exert an influence! Whether that is his intention is of no consequence; the thing is that he *can*.

FOR MORAL ENLIGHTENMENT

The Germans must be talked out of their Mephistopheles, and their Faust as well. These are two moral prejudices against the value of knowledge.

FAITH MAKES BLESSED

Virtue gives happiness and a kind of blessedness only to those who have faith in their virtue – though not to those subtler souls whose virtue consists in a profound distrust of themselves and in all virtue. Ultimately this too is 'faith' that makes 'blessed' – and *not*, mind you, virtue!

GUILT

Although the shrewdest judges of the witches, and even the witches themselves, were convinced that the latter were guilty of witchcraft, they were in fact guilty of nothing. So it is with all guilt.

FROM PARADISE

'Good and evil are the prejudices of God' – said the serpent.

WHAT MAKES YOU HEROIC?

To face at the same time your greatest suffering and your greatest hope.

WHAT DO YOU BELIEVE?

In this: that the weights of all things must be determined anew.

WHAT DOES YOUR CONSCIENCE SAY?

'You shall become who you are.'

WHAT IS YOUR GREATEST DANGER?

Pity.

WHAT DO YOU LOVE IN OTHERS?

My hopes.

WHOM DO YOU CALL BAD?

Those who always want to put others to shame.

WHAT IS MOST HUMANE?

To spare someone shame.

WHAT IS THE SEAL OF LIBERATION?

To no longer be ashamed of oneself.

PERSONAL PROVIDENCE

There is a certain high point in life, and once we have attained it, despite all the freedom we have won for ourselves, and the extent to which we deny that there is any benevolent reason or goodness in this beautiful chaos of an existence, we are once again confronted with the greatest threat to our intellectual freedom, and have to face our hardest test. It is only now that the thought of a personal providence impresses itself upon us with great force, having the best advocate, first-hand experience, to speak on its behalf, for it is a palpable fact that everything we encounter repeatedly *turns out for the best*. Every day and every hour, life seems to be eager for nothing more than to prove this proposition anew; whatever it may be, bad or good weather, the loss of a friend, an illness, a slander, a letter not arriving, a sprained ankle, a glance into a shop window, a counter-argument, the opening of a book, a dream, a swindle: it becomes apparent immediately, or shortly thereafter, that it was something 'indispensable' – something full of profound significance and advantage precisely *for us*! Is there anything besides such experiences which could so dangerously tempt us to dismiss the indifferent and unknowable gods of Epicurus, and believe instead in some anxious and petty divinity who personally knows every hair on our heads, and who has no aversion to rendering the most paltry of services? Well – all this notwithstanding, we wish to leave the gods in peace (and the serviceable genii as well), and to content ourselves with the assumption that our own practical and theoretical aptitude for the arrangement and explanation of events has now reached its zenith. We do not want to think too highly of our intellectual dexterity when the wonderful harmony which results from our playing on our instrument sometimes surprises even us: a harmony which sounds too good for us to dare to attribute it to ourselves. In fact, now and then, there is one who plays with us – our old friend chance; occasionally he leads us by the hand, and even an omniscient providence could not devise a finer music than that of which our foolish hand is then capable.

THE THOUGHT OF DEATH

It fills me with a melancholy happiness to live in the midst of this confusion of streets, of needs, of voices: how much enjoyment, impatience and desire, how much thirsty life and drunkenness of life comes into view here every day! And yet it will soon be so still for all these noisy people, the living with their thirst for life! Behold how behind every one of them stands his shadow, his dark companion! It is always like the final moment before a ship full of emigrants sets sail: people have more to say to one another than ever, the hour is pressing, the ocean and its desolate silence waits impatiently behind all the noise – so avid, so certain of its prey! And everyone, everyone thinks that what has gone before is little or nothing, that the near future is everything; hence all this haste, all this clamour, all this constant attempt to shout down and outwit one another! Everyone wants to be pre-eminent in this future – and yet death and the stillness of death are the only things that are certain and common to all in this future! How strange that this one certainty and commonality has almost no power over men, and that nothing is *further* from their minds than the brotherhood of death! I am glad that men try to avoid the thought of death altogether! I should like to do something to make the thought of life still a hundred times *more memorable.*

ARCHITECTURE FOR KNOWLEDGE-SEEKERS

We must recognize sooner or later that what is most lacking in our great cities are broad and spacious places for quiet reflection, places with long, lofty cloisters for when the weather is bad or all too sunny, where no sound of carriages or of town criers would penetrate, and where a more refined decorum would prohibit even the priest from praying aloud: buildings and facilities which as a whole would express the sublimity of contemplation and seclusion. The time is past when the Church can maintain a monopoly on reflection, when the *vita contemplativa* must first be the *vita religiosa*; but everything the Church has built expresses this thought. I do not know how we can be satisfied with their structures, even if they should be divested of their ecclesiastical purpose; these structures speak a far too declamatory and prejudiced language, as houses of God and gaudy places for supernatural intercourse, for us godless ones to be able to think *our thoughts* in them. We want to translate *ourselves* into stone and greenery, we want to walk *in ourselves* when we walk in these halls and gardens.

EXCELSIOR!

'You will never again pray, never again worship, never again rest in infinite trust – you refuse to stand and unharness your thoughts before an ultimate wisdom, an ultimate virtue, an ultimate power – you have no constant companion and friend for your seven solitudes – you live without a view of a mountain that has snow on its peak and fire in its heart – there is no longer anyone who will reward or punish for you, no longer anyone who will ultimately right wrongs for you – there is no longer any reason for what happens, or any love in what happens to you – there is no longer any resting place for your heart, where there is only finding and no more seeking, you resist any kind of ultimate peace, you desire the eternal recurrence of war and peace – man of renunciation, will you renounce all these things? Who will give you the strength to do so? No one has yet had this strength!'

There is a lake which one day failed to drain, for a dam was erected at the place where it had hitherto drained; since then this lake has been rising higher and higher. Perhaps this very renunciation will also furnish us with the strength with which the renunciation itself can be borne; perhaps from that point onwards man will rise higher and higher, when he no longer *drains* into a god.

ALL ABOARD!

When we consider how a complete philosophical justification of an individual's way of living and thinking affects him – namely, as a warming, blessing and fructifying sun, shining just for him; how it makes him independent of praise and blame, self-sufficient, rich and lavish in happiness and benevolence; how it continually transforms evil into good, brings all his powers to fruition and maturity and prevents the larger or smaller weeds of grief and despondency from springing up – in the end, we exclaim insistently: oh, that many such new suns might yet be created! Even the evil man, the unfortunate man, the exceptional man, should have his philosophy, his rights and his sunshine! They do not need our pity! We must unlearn this arrogant notion, no matter how long mankind has hitherto learned and practised it – no spiritual adviser, confessor or absolver needs to be established for them! Rather, a new *justice* is needed! And a new watchword! And new philosophers! The moral earth is also round! The moral earth also has its antipodes! The antipodes also have a right to exist! There is yet another world to discover – and more than one! All aboard, you philosophers!

TO THE PREACHERS OF MORALITY

I wish to preach no morality, but to those who do, I would give this advice: if you want to bring the best things and conditions into utter disrepute, continue to speak of them in the same manner as before! Place them at the head of your morality, and prattle on from morning till night about the pleasures of virtue, the repose of the soul, about justice, about inherent rewards and punishments; if you keep carrying on this way, all these good things will finally acquire popularity and a clamour in the streets for themselves; but then all the gold on the outside of them will wear off, and, what is more, all the gold on the *inside* will be transmuted into lead. Truly, you know how to practise alchemy in reverse, the devaluation of what is most valuable! Try just for once another recipe, in order to avoid bringing about opposite results from those you seek: *reject* those good things, deprive them of the applause of the mob and take them out of circulation, make them again the secret embarrassment of solitary souls, and say: *morality is something forbidden!* Perhaps you will thus gain for these things the only kind of men who are of any importance, by which I mean men who are *heroic*. But then there must be something fearsome about morality, and not, as hitherto, something disgusting! Where morality is concerned, might we not want to say today something similar to what was once said by Meister Eckhart: 'I ask God to make me free of God!'

AGAINST THE SLANDERERS
OF NATURE

They are such unpleasant people, these men in whom every natural inclination immediately becomes a disease, something disfiguring, or even disgraceful – it is *they* who have tempted us to think that men's inclinations and impulses are evil; *they* are the source of our great injustice towards our own nature, towards all nature! There are plenty of people who might yield to their impulses with grace and nonchalance; but they do not do so, for fear of that imaginary 'evil essence' in nature! *Hence* it has come to pass that there is so little nobility to be found among men; an indication of which will always be to fear nothing from oneself, to expect nothing disgraceful from oneself, to fly without hesitation wherever we are driven – we freeborn birds! Wherever we go, there will always be freedom and sunshine all around us.

ABILITY TO OPPOSE

Nowadays, everyone knows that the ability to brook opposition is a good indication of culture. Some even know that the superior man courts and provokes opposition, in order to discover his hitherto unknown biases. But the *ability* to oppose, to *not* have a bad conscience about being hostile towards the familiar, the traditional and the sacrosanct – that is more than both of them, that is the truly great, new and astonishing thing about our culture, and the most important step for the liberated spirit. But who knows that?

PRELUDES TO SCIENCE

Do you believe that the sciences would have arisen and grown if wizards, alchemists, astrologers and witches had not preceded them as those who, with their promises and pretences, had to create a thirst, a hunger and a taste for *hidden and forbidden* powers beforehand? Indeed, that infinitely more had to have been *promised* than could ever be fulfilled, if anything in the domain of knowledge were to be fulfilled at all?

Perhaps, just as these things proved to be preludes and preliminaries to science which were *not* practised and experienced as such, so too in some distant age the whole of *religion* may be regarded as an exercise and prelude; perhaps it will prove to have been the unlikely means by which individuals could enjoy the complete self-sufficiency of a god and all of his self-redeeming power. Indeed, one might ask: would man have ever learned to feel hunger and thirst for *himself*, and to derive satisfaction and abundance from *himself*, without that religious schooling and prehistory? Did Prometheus have to first *imagine* that he had *stolen* the light and atoned for that, in order to discover in the end that he had created the light *by coveting the light*, and that not only man, but

God too had been the work of his hands and the clay in his hands? That all of it had been mere images in the mind of the imaginative individual, creations in the mind of the creator? And likewise the delusion, the theft, the Caucasus, the vulture and the whole tragic *Prometheia* of all knowledge-seekers?

SELF-MASTERY

Those moral teachers who first and foremost insist that man exercise self-control thereby subject him to a peculiar affliction – namely, a constant irritability with regard to all natural impulses and inclinations, and, as it were, a kind of itching. Henceforth, whatever may goad, pull, attract or impel him, whether from within or from without – it always seems to this irritable being as if his self-mastery were in danger: he may no longer entrust himself to any of his instincts, to any free beating of his wings, but must constantly adopt a defensive posture, armed against himself, with keen and distrustful eyes, the eternal guardian of the castle into which he has made himself. Yes, he can achieve *greatness* in this way! But how insufferable he has now become to others, how hard to bear even for himself, how impoverished and deprived of the most beautiful contingencies of the soul! Yes, even of all further *instruction*! From time to time we must be able to lose ourselves, if we wish to learn from the things which are not ourselves.

IN FAVOUR OF CRITICISM

Something now strikes you as an error which you had formerly loved as a truth, or at least as a probability; you shed the opinion and imagine that your reason has thereby gained a victory. But perhaps you were a different person then – at any given moment you are a different person – and at that time the error was necessary for you, just as necessary for you as all your present 'truths' are. It was like a skin, as it were, which covered and concealed from you much that you were not yet allowed to see. Your new life, not your rationality, has killed that opinion for you: *you did not need it any more*, and now it has broken down of its own accord, and its irrationality has crawled out of it like a worm into the light. When we engage in criticism it is nothing voluntary or impersonal – it is, or at least very often it is, proof that there are vital, driving forces in us which are shedding a skin. We negate and must negate because something in us lives and *wants* to affirm itself, perhaps something we are as yet unfamiliar with, perhaps something we are as yet unable to see! This speaks in favour of criticism.

Friedrich Nietzsche

NO IMAGES OF MARTYRS

I will follow the example of Raphael, and never again paint an image of a martyr. There are enough sublime things in the world already for us to have to seek the sublime where it lives as a sister to cruelty. I have a greater ambition, and it is not enough for me to make myself into a sublime torturer.

AS INTERPRETERS OF OUR EXPERIENCES

One form of honesty has always been lacking among founders of religions and the like – they have never made their experiences a matter of intellectual conscience. 'What did I actually experience? What took place just then within me and around me? Was my reason clear enough? Was I sufficiently determined to resist every deception of the senses, and resolute in repelling anything fantastic?' None of them ever asked these questions, nor have any of our good religious people yet asked them. Rather, they have a thirst for things which are *contrary to reason*, and they do not want it to be too difficult to satisfy this thirst – so they experience 'miracles' and 'rebirths', and hear the voices of angels! But we who are different, who are thirsty for reason, want to look as rigorously at our experiences as if they were scientific experiments, hour after hour, day after day! We ourselves want to be our experiments and our experimental animals.

NEW PRECAUTION

Let us no longer think so much about punishment, blame and improvement! We seldom change an individual, and when we do succeed, perhaps something else occurs without our realizing it: he may have succeeded in changing *us*! Rather, let us see to it that our own influence *on all that is to come* offsets and outweighs his influence! Let us refrain from direct conflict – and that includes all blame, punishment and desire for improvement! Instead, let us elevate ourselves that much higher! Let us make ourselves an ever more shining example! Let our light put others in the shade! No! We do not wish to become *darker* ourselves on his account, like all who punish and are dissatisfied! Let us stand aside! Let us look away!

A SIMILE

Those thinkers in whom all the planets move in circular orbits are not the most profound. He who looks into himself, as into an immense space, and carries Milky Ways within himself, also knows how irregular all Milky Ways are: they lead into the chaos and labyrinth of existence.

IN MEDIA VITA

No! Life has not deceived or disappointed me! Every year I find it more genuine, more desirable and more mysterious – ever since the day when the great liberator came to me: the idea that life might be an experiment for the knowledge-seeker – and not a duty, not a tragedy, not a swindle!

For others, knowledge itself may be something else: for example, a day bed, or the way to a day bed, or an entertainment, or a diversion – for me, it is a world of dangers and victories in which even the heroic sentiments have their place, and are free to dance and romp about. *'Life as a means to knowledge'* – with this principle in one's heart one can not only live bravely, but can even *live joyously and laugh joyously*! And who would know how to laugh well and live well, if he did not first know war and victory well?

PHYSICIANS OF THE SOUL AND PAIN

All preachers of morality, like all theologians, have a bad habit in common: all of them try to persuade man that he is in a very bad way, and that a severe, ultimate, radical cure is necessary. And because mankind as a whole has too eagerly lent its ears to these doctrines for centuries, men have come to believe something of the superstition that things are going quite badly, so that they are now far too ready to sigh; they no longer find life worth living and make sad faces at one another as if it were difficult to *bear*. In truth, they are irrepressibly sanguine about their lives and in love with them, and unspeakably cunning and subtle at ridding themselves of anything unpleasant, and taking the sting out of pain and misfortune. It seems to me that people always *exaggerate* when it comes to pain and misfortune, as if one were expected to exaggerate here. On the other hand, people are deliberately silent about the fact that there are innumerable palliatives for pain: anaesthesia; a feverish rush of thought; a restful posture; good or bad memories, intentions and hopes; many kinds of pride and sympathy which have almost the effect of anaesthetics; and, with the most extreme pains, falling into a swoon. We know all too well how to sprinkle a little sweetness over our bitterness, especially over the bitterness of the soul; we find expedients in our bravery and sublimity, as well as in the nobler deliria of submission and resignation. A loss is hardly a loss for an hour:

somehow a gift from heaven falls into our lap with it – a new form of strength, for example – even if it is only a new opportunity to exercise strength! What fantastical ideas have the preachers of morality not entertained concerning the inner 'misery' of evil men! How they have *deceived* us about the misfortunes of passionate men! Yes, deceit is the right word here: they were all too aware of the superabundant happiness of this kind of man, but they were as silent as the grave about it, because it refuted their theory that happiness is the result of the extinction of the passions and the silencing of the will! And as far as the recipe of all these physicians of the soul is concerned, and their touting of a severely radical cure, might we be allowed to ask: is our life really painful and irksome enough for it to be worthwhile for us to exchange it for a Stoical way of life, and Stoical petrification? Our lives are *not miserable enough* for us to have to be miserable the way that Stoics are!

HURRAH FOR PHYSICS!

How many people know how to observe? And of the few who do – how many observe themselves? 'No one is a neighbour to himself' – all the triers of the reins know this, much to their chagrin; and the saying, 'know thyself', in the mouth of a god and spoken to man, borders on cruelty. But nothing better demonstrates that matters are desperate with regard to self-observation than the manner in which *almost everybody* speaks about the essence of a moral action, this immediate, unhesitating, convinced, voluble manner, with its characteristic look, smile and agreeable enthusiasm! They seem to want to say, 'But, my dear chap, that is precisely *my* métier! You have addressed your question to one who is *particularly well qualified* to speak upon just the subject, for as luck would have it, there is nothing about which I am more informed! So, when a man judges that "*this is right*", accordingly concludes that "*therefore it must be done*", and then *does* what he has thus recognized was right and indicated was necessary – then the essence of his action is *moral*!' 'But, my good man, you are talking about three actions instead of one: for example, your judgement that "this is right" is also an action – might we not judge in a moral or immoral way? *Why* do you consider this in particular to be right?' 'Because my conscience tells me so; conscience never speaks immorally, indeed it determines what is moral in the first place!' But why do you *listen* to the voice of conscience? And to what extent are you entitled to regard such a judgement as true and unmistakable? This *faith* of yours – must it not also be examined conscientiously? Do you know nothing of the intellectual conscience? A conscience which comes along after your 'conscience'? Your judgement 'this is right' has a prior history in your impulses, in your inclinations and disinclinations, in what you have experienced and in what you have not experienced; first you must ask: *where* did it come from? And then ask: *what* really impels me to listen to it? You can listen to its command like a brave soldier listening to his commanding officer. Or like a woman in love with the man who commands her. Or like a flatterer and a coward who is afraid of the commander. Or like a numbskull who obeys because no objection has occurred to him. In short, you can listen to your conscience in a hundred different ways. But *the mere fact that* you hear this or that judgement as the voice of conscience, and that consequently you feel a thing to be right, may be due to the fact that you have never given the matter much thought, and have blindly accepted from your childhood whatever you were *told* was right; or it may be due to the fact that, hitherto, the enjoyment of bread and honours has been part and parcel of the thing which you call your duty – it seems 'right' to you, because it seems to be a 'condition of *your* existence' (and the notion that you have a *right* to exist strikes you as indisputable!). The *firmness* of your moral judgement may be nothing more than proof of your personal in-adequacy, of your lack of character; your 'moral fortitude' might have its source in your stubbornness – or in your lack of ability to envision new ideals! And, to be brief: if you had thought more carefully, observed more closely and had learned more, you would no longer call this and that your 'duty' and your 'conscience' under any circumstances; insight into *how moral judgements arise at all* would spoil for you these lofty words – just as these other lofty words have already been spoiled for you, words like 'sin', 'salvation' and 'redemption'.

Now, my good man, do not give me any of that nonsense about the categorical imperative! That phrase tickles my ear, and I must laugh despite your earnestness in my presence. I am reminded of old Kant, who, as a punishment for having *fraudulently obtained* the 'thing in itself' – also a rather ridiculous notion! – arrived at the notion of the categorical imperative, and with that in his heart, *wandered back* into the notions of God, the soul, freedom and immortality, like a fox who inadvertently wanders back into his own cage – when it was his strength and cunning which had *broken* this cage wide open!

How is that? You admire the categorical impera-tive within you? This 'firmness' of your so-called moral judgement? This 'unconditionality' of the feeling that 'as I judge, so must everyone judge'? Rather, admire your *selfishness* in feeling that way! And the blind, petty and unassuming nature of your selfishness! It is selfishness to consider one's *own* judgement a universal law, and a blind, petty and unassuming selfishness besides, for it betrays that you have not yet discovered yourself, that you have not yet created an ideal of your own, entirely your own – such an ideal could never be shared with another, let alone with everyone, everyone! Whoever still judges that 'in this case, everyone must act in this manner' has not yet advanced five steps in self-knowledge; otherwise he would know that there neither are, nor can there be, identical actions. Every action that has ever been done, has been done in an entirely unique and unprecedented manner, and the same will be true of all future actions. Every prescription with regard to our actions (even the most subtle and inward prescriptions of every moral code hitherto) applies only to their rough exterior, and while these prescriptions may convey the impression that there are identical cases, such an impression is *misleading*. *Every* action, whether viewed prospectively or retrospectively, is and remains impenetrable. Our opinions with regard to 'goodness', 'nobility' or 'greatness' can never be *demonstrated* by our actions, because every action is unknowable, and while our opinions, value judgements and standards of goodness are certainly among the most powerful levers in the machinery of our actions, in any individual instance the law of their mechanism is indeterminable. Let us *confine* ourselves, therefore, to the purification of our opinions and value judgements, and to the creation of our own original standards of goodness – but let us no longer brood over the 'moral worth of our actions'! Yes, my friends! The time has come for us to turn away in disgust from all this nonsense of some standing in moral judgement over others! The whole thing is in such bad taste! Let us leave this nonsense and this bad taste to those who have nothing better to do than to keep the past alive a little bit longer and who never live in the here and now – let us leave them to the many, to the great majority! We, however, *want to become who we are* – something new, unique, incomparable, self-legislating and self-creating! And to that end, we must become the best students and discoverers of all the laws and necessities in the world. We must be *physicists* in order to be *creators* in that sense – whereas hitherto all value judgements and ideals have been based on an ignorance of physics, or in contradiction with it. And so I say, hurrah for physics! And an even louder hurrah for that which impels us to it – our honesty.

Friedrich Nietzsche

THE WILLINGNESS TO SUFFER
AND THE PITYING

Is it beneficial for you to be filled with pity above all
else? And is it beneficial to those who suffer for you
to be filled with pity? But let us leave the first question unanswered for a moment.

The things from which we suffer most deeply
and personally are almost incomprehensible and
inaccessible to anybody but ourselves; in this, we are
hidden from our neighbour even when we eat from
the same pot. But whenever we are *perceived* to be
suffering, our suffering is viewed superficially; it is
essential to the emotion of pity that it *divest* the
suffering of a stranger of its underlying personal
character – 'do-gooders' diminish our value and
disregard our intentions more than our enemies do.
In most of the good deeds which are done for the
unfortunate there is something outrageous about
the intellectual frivolity with which the pitying person assumes the role of Fortune: he knows nothing
of the totality of the inner consequences and inter-
connections which he calls unhappiness in *my* case
or in *yours*! The whole economy of my soul and its
tempering by 'unhappiness', the emergence of new
sources and needs, the healing of old wounds, the

discarding of whole past histories – none of the things which might be associated with unhappiness are of the least concern to our dear friend, the pitying person. He merely wishes to help and does not take into account the fact that we have a personal need for unhappiness; that terror, deprivation, impoverishment, midnights of the soul, adventures, risks and mistakes are as necessary to you and me as their opposites; indeed, that, to speak mystically, the way to one's own heaven always leads through the voluptuousness of one's own hell. No, he knows nothing about that. The 'religion of pity' (or 'the heart') dictates that he help, and he thinks he has helped most when he has helped fastest! If you disciples of this religion actually have the same attitude towards yourselves as you have towards your fellows, if you are not willing to endure your own suffering even for an hour, and are always trying to avoid every unhappy experience you can, if you generally regard pain and sorrow as evil, as detestable, as deserving of destruction, as a blot on existence – well then, besides your religion of pity, you have yet another religion in your heart (which is perhaps the mother of the former): *the religion of comfortableness*. Oh how little you know about human *happiness*, you comfortable and good-natured people – for happiness and unhappiness are sisters and twins which grow tall together, or, in your case, *remain small* together! But now let us return to the first question.

How is it even possible for a man to keep to his *own* path! Things are incessantly clamouring for our attention; we rarely see anything which does not require us to drop everything instantly and rush to somebody's assistance. I know how it is: there are hundreds of respectable and commendable ways of making me *lose my way* and, in truth, all of them highly 'moral' ways! Indeed, the contemporary preachers of this morality of pity even go so far as to say that this alone is moral – to lose *our* way so that we might better rush to our neighbour's assistance. I likewise know for certain that I need only surrender myself to the sight of someone in genuine distress, and I *am* lost! And if a suffering friend said to me, 'Look, soon I am going to die; promise you will die with me', I would promise it, just as the sight of a small mountain tribe fighting for its freedom would make me offer them my hand and my life – to choose bad examples for good reasons. Indeed, there is even a secret temptation in all this arousing of pity, in all these cries for help: our 'own way' is too difficult and demanding, and too far removed from the love and gratitude of others – we are not at all disinclined to run away from it and our own conscience, and to flee into the conscience of others, taking refuge in the lovely temple of the 'religion of pity'. Every time a war breaks out, a desire invariably breaks out at the same time among precisely the noblest people in the nation, though they are naturally loath to disclose it: they enthusiastically throw themselves into this new risk of *death* because they believe that by sacrificing themselves for their country they have finally obtained the permission which they have long sought – the permission to *abandon their aims*; war is for them a detour to suicide, but a detour with a good conscience. And although I prefer to remain silent here about some things, I will not remain silent about my morality, which says to me: live in obscurity so that you are *able* to live for yourself! Live in *ignorance* of that which is most important to your age! Put at least the skin of three centuries between yourself and today! And the clamour of today, the noise of wars and revolutions, shall be to you but a murmur! You will also want to help, but only help those whose distress you fully *understand*, because they share with you one sorrow and one hope – your *friends*; and only in the same way that you would help yourself – for I want to make them more courageous, more steadfast, more simple, more joyous! I want to teach them the importance of something which so few seem to

understand these days, and which the preachers of
pity, the preachers of shared sorrow, seem to understand least of all – the importance of *shared joy*!

WHAT OUR CHEERFULNESS MEANS

The greatest event of recent times – the fact that
'God is dead', that the belief in the Christian God
has become untenable – has already begun to cast
its first shadows over Europe. For the few at least
whose eyes, whose *suspicious* eyes, are strong enough
and subtle enough for this drama, some sun seems
to have set, some ancient and profound confidence has turned into doubt; to these eyes our old
world must seem to be becoming more vespertine,
distrustful, strange and 'old' with every passing day.
In the main, however, we may say that the event
itself is much too great, too remote, too far beyond
most people's capacity to understand, for us to
imagine that even the tidings of it could have *reached*
their ears, let alone that very many people would
already know *what* its actual implications were, or
what things would have to collapse, now that this
belief had been undermined, because they were
built upon it, leaned against it and had become inter-
twined with it: for example, our entire European
morality. With regard to this long and abundant

train of consequences which are now imminent, this demolition and destruction, this decline and fall, who nowadays has already divined enough of it to have to play the educator and prognosticator of this tremendous logic of terror, to play the prophet of a gloom and solar eclipse the like of which has probably never before existed on earth?

Even we natural-born speculators who, so to speak, wait on the mountains, posted between today and tomorrow, spanning the contradiction between today and tomorrow, we firstlings and premature births of the coming century for whom the shadows which, incidentally, *should* have arrived by now, the shadows which must soon afterwards envelop Europe – how is it that we ourselves await its advent without properly participating in this gloom, without any concern or fear for *ourselves*? Perhaps we stand too close to the *immediate consequences* of this event – and these immediate consequences, its consequences for *ourselves*, are the reverse of what one might have expected, they are by no means sad and gloomy, but rather like a new and indescribable kind of light, happiness, relief, amusement, encouragement and dawn . . .

In fact, we philosophers and 'free spirits' experience the news that the 'old God is dead' as if illuminated by a new dawn; our hearts are overflowing with gratitude, astonishment, presentiment and expectation – at last the horizon seems free again, even if it is not bright; at last our ships can set sail again, ready to face every danger; every venture of the knowledge-seeker is permitted again; the sea, *our* sea, lies open again before us; perhaps there has never been such an 'open sea'.

TO WHAT EXTENT EVEN
WE ARE STILL PIOUS

It is said with good reason that convictions have no civil rights in science: it is only when they are willing to reduce themselves to the humble status of a hypothesis, of a preliminary experimental standpoint, of a regulative fiction, that they may be allowed to enter the domain of knowledge, and even be accorded a certain value within it – though with the proviso that they must be kept under constant surveillance, under the surveillance of our distrust.

But does that not imply that, strictly speaking, a conviction may gain admission to science only when it *ceases* to be a conviction? Does not the discipline of the scientific spirit only begin when we are no longer allowed any convictions?

Very probably; but it remains to be seen whether there does not have to be some sort of conviction present in the first place *in order for this discipline to begin*, a conviction so imperative and unconditional that it makes us sacrifice all our other convictions. We see that even science rests upon a faith, that there is no 'presuppositionless' science. The question of whether *truth* is necessary must not only be answered in the affirmative beforehand, it must be answered in the affirmative to such an extent that the principle, faith or conviction is expressed that '*nothing* is more necessary than truth, in comparison to which everything else is of only secondary importance'.

This unconditional determination to seek the truth: what is it? Is it the determination *not to be deceived*? Is it the determination *not to deceive*? For the desire for truth could also be interpreted in this fashion, provided that under the generalization 'I will not deceive' one subsumed the individual case, 'I will not deceive myself.' But why not deceive? Why not allow oneself to be deceived?

It should be noted that the reasons for the former are quite different from the reasons for the latter: we wish not to be deceived on the assumption that it is harmful, dangerous or disastrous to be deceived – in this sense, science would be a long exercise of prudence and caution, essentially utilitarian in its nature, against which we might however reasonably object: 'What? Is wishing-not-to-be-deceived really less harmful, less dangerous, less disastrous?' What do you know from the outset about the character of existence that enables you to determine whether the greater advantage is on the side of unconditional distrust or unconditional trust? But if both a great deal of trust and a great deal of distrust should prove necessary, then from where would science derive its unconditional faith, the conviction on which it rests, that truth is more important than anything else, more important even than every other conviction? It is precisely this conviction that could not have arisen if truth *and* untruth had both constantly proved themselves to be useful, as is the case. Thus the faith in science, which now undeniably exists, cannot have originated in such a utilitarian calculation, but rather in spite of the fact that the uselessness and dangerousness of the 'desire for truth', for 'truth at any cost', are constantly being demonstrated. 'At any cost': oh, we understand that well enough, after having offered and slaughtered one faith after another on this altar!

Consequently, 'desire for truth' does not mean 'I do not want to be deceived', but – there is no other alternative – 'I will not deceive, not even myself' – *and with that we have reached the ground of morality.* For we have to ask ourselves searchingly: 'Why not deceive?', especially if it should seem – and it does seem – as if life aims at appearance, I mean, at error, deception, dissimulation, delusion, self-delusion; and when, on the other hand, life in its broad outlines has always shown itself to be on the side of the most unscrupulous *polytropoi*. It might be the case that such an intention is, to put it mildly, quixotic, a piece of enthusiastic madness; but it might also be something much worse, namely a destructive principle, a principle hostile to life . . . 'the desire for truth' might well be a concealed desire for death . . .

Thus the question 'Why have science at all?' leads back to the moral problem: *why have morality at all* when life, nature and history are 'immoral'? There is no doubt that the truthful man in the daring and extreme sense of that word, the man whose truthfulness is presupposed by science, *thereby affirms another world*, a world that transcends life, nature and history; and in so far as he affirms this 'other world' – what? Does he not have to *negate* its counterpart, this world, our world?

But you understand what I am driving at, namely that it is still a *metaphysical faith* on which our faith in science rests – and that even we knowledge-seekers of the present day, we godless anti-metaphysicians, light *our* fire from the flames enkindled by a faith which goes back thousands of years, that Christian faith which was also the faith of Plato, that God is truth, that truth is divine . . .

But what if this faith is becoming ever more incredible; what if nothing proves to be more divine than error, blindness and falsehood – what if God Himself should prove to be our most longest-lasting lie?

MORALITY AS A PROBLEM

A personal defect takes its revenge everywhere; an enfeebled, slight, self-effacing and self-denying personality is no longer good for anything – least of all for philosophy. 'Selflessness' has no value in heaven or on earth; great problems all demand *great love* and it is only the frank, strong, self-confident spirits with steady nerves who are at all proficient with them. It makes a considerable difference whether a thinker takes his problems personally, finding in them his destiny, his distress and even his greatest happiness; or merely 'impersonally', that is to say, if he can only grasp and comprehend them with little feelers of cold and inquisitive thought. In the latter case nothing comes of it, I can assure you, for the great problems, assuming that they can be grasped at all, *elude the grasp* of toads and weaklings; that has been their taste since time began – a taste, by the way, which they share with all doughty women.

How is it that I have not yet come across anyone, not even in books, whose position regarding morality was that of a person who knew that morality was a problem, and who experienced this problem as *his own* personal distress, torment, voluptuousness and passion? It is evident that hitherto morality has been no problem at all; rather, it was the one thing on which people could agree, despite all distrust, dissension and disagreement, a holy sanctuary where thinkers catch their breath, recuperate and take a rest even from themselves. I see no one who would have dared to *criticize* moral value judgements. I have found such a thing completely lacking; there is not even an attempt at scientific curiosity, or the fastidious, experimental imagination of psychologists and historians, which easily anticipates a problem and catches it in flight, without really knowing what it has caught. I have hardly been able to locate a few rudiments of a *developmental history* of the origin of these sentiments and value judgements (which is something other than a criticism of them, and also something other than a history of ethical systems); in an individual case I have done all I could to encourage the inclination and aptitude for this kind of history – in vain, as it now appears. Little can be done with these historians of morality (especially the English); usually they themselves are still unwittingly under the direction of a particular morality, and without realizing it serve as its standard-bearers and hangers-on: for example, that popular superstition of Christian Europe which is still faithfully parroted everywhere that the characteristic of moral action consists in selflessness, self-denial, self-sacrifice, or in sympathy and pity. Their usual mistaken assumption is the claim that some kind of consensus exists among peoples, or at least civilized peoples, regarding certain propositions of morality, and that therefore these propositions are unconditionally binding even upon you and me; or, after the truth has been revealed to them that moral value judgements *necessarily* differ among different peoples, they conversely come to the conclusion that *no* morality is binding – which are both equally childish. The error of the more discerning among them is to discover and criticize the possibly foolish opinions of a people about its own morality, or of mankind about human morality in general – that is, about its origin, its religious sanctions, the superstition of free will and the like – and think that precisely by doing so they have criticized the morality itself. But the value of the prescription 'thou shalt' is fundamentally different from and independent of such opinions about it, and from the weeds of error with which it might be overgrown; just as the value of a medicine to a patient is completely independent of whether the patient thinks scientifically about medicine or fills his head with old wives' tales. A morality could even be the outgrowth of an error; but with this insight the problem of its value is not even touched upon.

So far, no one has examined the *value* of that most famous of all medicines called morality, to which end one must first *call it into question*. Well, that is precisely our work.

OUR QUESTION MARK

But you do not understand that? As a matter of fact, there is no small difficulty in understanding us. We are endeavouring to find the words in which to express ourselves; perhaps we are also endeavouring to find the ears with which others might hear them. Who are we, though? If we wanted simply to refer to ourselves by the older expressions, atheists, unbelievers or even immoralists, we would still be far from believing that those words adequately described us; we are all of those things in such an advanced condition that no one fully grasps our state of mind, indeed, no one is even *able* to grasp it, not even *you*, my inquisitive friends. No, we no longer suffer from the bitterness and passion of the man who has just broken free, and who has to create for himself a faith, a goal and a martyrdom even, out of his unbelief! We know full well (and have become cold and severe in the realization) that the world is not at all divine, indeed, that it is not even humanly rational, merciful or just; we know that the world in which we live is ungodly, immoral and 'inhuman' – for far too long we have interpreted it falsely and dishonestly, in accordance with our wish and intention to revere it, that is to say, according to a *need*. After all, man is a reverent animal! But he is also a distrustful one; and in the end, the fact that the world is *not* as valuable as we had believed is about the surest thing that our distrust has got hold of. And the more distrust, the more philosophy! However, we must be careful not to say that the world is any *less* valuable than it should be; it now seems ludicrous to us whenever man claims that he has devised values which are supposed to *surpass* the value of the real world – it is precisely from that idea that we have retreated as from an extravagant aberration, a piece of human vanity and irrationality which for a long time has not been recognized as such. It had its most recent expression in modern pessimism, and an older and stronger one in the teachings of the Buddha; but Christianity also contains it, more uncertainly of course, and more ambiguously, but no less seductively on that account. The whole posture of 'man *against* the world', man as 'world-denying' principle, man as the value standard for everything, a judge of the world who ultimately places existence itself on the scales and finds it wanting – we have become aware of the tremendous vulgarity of this posture and it disgusts us; we now laugh when we find 'man *and* world' juxtaposed, separated by the sublime presumption of that little word 'and'! How is that? Have we not by laughing taken our contempt for mankind one step further? And therefore also our pessimism, our contempt for any existence which is recognizable by *us*? Have we not in just this way become smitten with the suspicion that there is an antithesis between the familiar world of our reverences – reverences which may have rendered life *bearable* – and another world which we ourselves are: an implacable and profound suspicion about ourselves which is only getting worse and worse, and by which we Europeans in particular are increasingly swayed, the deepest suspicion which might easily confront the coming generation with a terrible alternative:

either eliminate your reverences or – eliminate yourselves! The latter would be nihilism – but would not the former also be nihilism? This is *our* question mark.

BELIEVERS AND THEIR NEED OF BELIEF

How much *belief* someone needs in order to prosper, how many 'firmly held opinions' he needs which he does not want to have shaken, because he is *attached* to them – is a measure of his strength (or, to put it more clearly, of his weakness). It seems to me that Christianity is still regarded as necessary in old Europe, and so it still finds believers. For man is such that a theological dogma might be refuted a thousand times, but if he had need of it he would always accept it as 'true', according to the famous 'demonstration of power' of which the Bible speaks. Some individuals still have need of metaphysics; but also that vehement *longing for certainty* which nowadays discharges itself in the general populace in a scientific and positivistic manner, the longing to possess something absolutely firm (a longing which, because of its fervour, leads to casual and negligent attempts at substantiating the certainty) – this too is nothing but the longing for some kind of foothold or support; in short, it is that *instinct of weakness* which does not actually create religious beliefs, metaphysical ideas and convictions of all kinds, but rather conserves them. In fact, a certain air of pessimistic gloom hangs over all these positivist systems, a sense of weariness, fatalism, disillusionment and fear of further disillusionment – or else a great show of ire, ill-humour, anarchistic indignation and all the other symptoms whereby the sense of weakness masquerades as something else. Even the vehemence with which our cleverest contemporaries lose themselves in wretched corners and alleyways, for example, in fatherlandery (that is, what in France is called *chauvinisme* and in Germany is called 'German'); or in obscure aesthetic denominations in the manner of Parisian *naturalisme* (which only brings out and lays bare that aspect of nature which excites disgust and at the same time astonishment – nowadays they like to call this aspect *la vérité vraie*); or in nihilism of the St Petersburg variety (that is to say, in the *belief in unbelief*, even to the point of martyrdom for it) – this always shows itself first and foremost in the *need* for a belief, foothold, backbone or buttress . . .

Belief is always most desired, is most urgently necessary, where will is lacking; for the will, as the passion of imperiousness, is the distinguishing characteristic of self-mastery and strength. That is to say, the less someone is able to command, the more urgently he desires someone to command him, and command him strictly – a god, a prince, a caste, a physician, a confessor, a dogma, the conscience of a party. From which we might deduce that what accounts for the origin of the two world religions Buddhism and Christianity, and their sudden spread in particular, was a tremendous *disease of the will*. And so it was: both religions discovered a longing for just such a 'thou shalt', attributable to an absurdly large increase in this disease which had driven people to the brink of despair; both religions taught fanaticism in those periods when atony of the will was prevalent, and thereby offered to innumerable people a foothold, a new opportunity for willing, an enjoyment of the will. For fanaticism is actually the only 'strength of will' of which the weak and irresolute are capable, as a kind of hypnotizing of the entire sensory-intellectual system, an excessive preoccupation with, and hypertrophy of, a particular point of view and a particular sentiment which then comes to dominate them – the Christian calls it his *belief*. When a man arrives at the fundamental conviction that he must be commanded, he becomes a 'believer'; conversely, we could imagine a delight in and capacity for self-determination, a *freedom* of will, by which a spirit bids farewell to every belief, to every wish for certainty, being proficient in hanging on to thin ropes and possibilities, and even in dancing on the brink of the abyss. Such a spirit would be the *free spirit* par excellence.